Praise for *The Seven Skins*
Booktopia's 2022 Book

'This intercontinental journey into joy, grief, nature and magic confirms Holly Ringland as one of Australia's most precious, life-changing storytellers' – Booktopia

'A mythological journey as much as an unfolding mystery, full of symbols … a magical, witchy, quirky, luminous book, full of the natural world, the night sky and the ever-changing water around the islands on which it is set' – *The Australian*

'Like the best books, *The Seven Skins of Esther Wilding* is ultimately a story about love. Ringland is a virtuoso of fairytale storytelling for adults' – *Sydney Morning Herald*

'Fans of Holly Ringland's beautiful first novel, *The Lost Flowers of Alice Hart*, will fall equally in love with her second' – *West Australian*

'Vivid and soaring … evocative … a haunting story of trauma and redemption that is nonetheless compelling and accessible. It's a great recommendation for fans of Vanessa Diffenbaugh's *The Language of Flowers* or Elizabeth Gilbert's *The Signature of All Things*, as well as Ringland's debut, *The Lost Flowers of Alice Hart*' – *Books+Publishing*

'A magical novel about loss, grief and new beginnings' – Mamamia

'Holly Ringland creates expansive magical worlds in her novels and packs them full of love. The story of Esther Wilding will get under your skin and stay there well after the last page' – Victoria Hannan, author of *Kokomo* and *Marshmallow*

'Myths and legends are the touchstone to truth in this epic journey through love, loss, courage and kinship. But *The Seven Skins of Esther Wilding* is also an elegant and mesmerising tribute to the places that hold our stories, heart and memories. Holly Ringland writes with such tenderness, wit and imagination about all these things that it's impossible to come away from this magical story unchanged' – Sally Piper, author of *Bone Memories*

'Another spell is cast by Holly Ringland. I was swept away by this triumphant and luminous story' – Myfanwy Jones, Miles Franklin Literary Award shortlisted author for *Leap*

'Nobody writes about the pain of being alive more deftly than Holly Ringland. She brings such empathy to the topics of grief, love, family conflict and loss. Some of her sentences took my breath away, and I found myself madly flicking pages, days later, to find them again for safekeeping. Astonishing in its scope, detail and sensitivity, *The Seven Skins of Esther Wilding* is tender, magical, epic, funny and devastating. This is a very special writer at her best' – Kate Leaver, author of *The Friendship Cure*

Praise for *The Lost Flowers of Alice Hart*

'A dark, floral fairytale ... There is a reason Ringland's novel, her first, and already a bestseller, has been bought by publishers around the world, and it's not the native flowers ... The first half of *The Lost Flowers* is delicate and dark as a fairytale, with violent details that stick to you like burrs. But it is in the second half, with Alice out in the real world, where Ringland really gets into gear, and her talent is undeniable ... Ringland's storytelling is driven by an undimmed sense of wonder at the darkness and light, the damage and love in people. It makes for a determined investigation of abuse and survival accomplished with profound sensitivity' – *Sydney Morning Herald*

'Domestic violence and the lies that surround it – rarely is the topic explored in such a beautifully written, hopeful and enthralling tale' – *Herald Sun*

'Lush, powerful ... This is an engrossing novel imbued with passion and reverence for the Australian natural world, with a cast of characters that inspire affection in the reader even as they make mistakes. Those who couldn't put down *The Natural Way of Things* will find a gentler but no less compelling journey of female survival in this novel' – *Books+Publishing*

'There's an aching heart beating through Holly Ringland's narrative that although at times seems almost broken, is stitched back together with shards of optimism that offer constant hope. These are characters we love, care about and want to nurture ... A vivid and brave tale of love, loss and inner power' – *Australian Women's Weekly*

'At its heart, this book is about finding a way to care for yourself, in a world that sometimes likes to step on its flowers' – *Courier-Mail*

HOLLY RINGLAND is the author of the international bestseller *The Lost Flowers of Alice Hart*, which has been translated into thirty languages and adapted into a seven-part TV series starring Sigourney Weaver, produced by Amazon Prime and Made Up Stories. In 2019, *The Lost Flowers of Alice Hart* won the Australian Book Industry Award General Fiction Book of the Year. In 2021, Holly co-hosted an eight-episode ABC TV series, *Back to Nature*, with Aaron Pedersen. After living between Australia and the UK for ten years, Holly has been based in the Yugambeh region of southeast Queensland since 2020, where she wrote her second novel, *The Seven Skins of Esther Wilding*, in her 'office', a vintage caravan named Frenchie.

Upon publication, *The Seven Skins of Esther Wilding* became an instant national bestseller, and it was named Booktopia's 2022 Book of the Year.

WWW.HOLLYRINGLAND.COM

The House That Joy Built

HOLLY RINGLAND

FOURTH ESTATE

Fourth Estate
An imprint of HarperCollins*Publishers*

HarperCollins*Publishers*
Australia • Brazil • Canada • France • Germany • Holland • India
Italy • Japan • Mexico • New Zealand • Poland • Spain • Sweden
Switzerland • United Kingdom • United States of America

HarperCollins acknowledges the Traditional Custodians
of the land upon which we live and work, and pays respect
to Elders past and present.

First published on Gadigal Country in Australia in 2023
This edition published in 2025
by HarperCollins*Publishers* Australia Pty Limited
ABN 36 009 913 517
harpercollins.com.au

A catalogue record for this book is available from the National Library of Australia

ISBN 978 1 4607 6703 0 (paperback)
ISBN 978 1 4607 1663 2 (ebook)
ISBN 978 1 4607 3428 5 (audiobook)

Cover and internal design by Hazel Lam, HarperCollins Design Studio
Cover illustration © Kate Dehler Illustration, LLC
Internal illustrations by Edith Rewa
Author photograph by Michelle Larson
Typeset in Bembo Std by Kirby Jones
Printed and bound in Australia by McPherson's Printing Group

MIX
Paper from
responsible sources
FSC
www.fsc.org   FSC® C001695

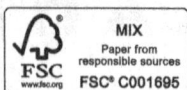

To the wild mystery of our ideas.
Those we've dared to honour and make.
And those waiting, impatiently, for us to create.

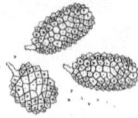

CONTENTS

I am out with lanterns,
looking for myself.

EMILY DICKINSON

A Light Left On

The morning dawns in England and I am woken by the purple light. It's winter 2014. I'm thirty-four years old. I lie in bed and stare out of the window. My body feels too heavy, as if there's a second skeleton under my skin with bones made not of calcium but of fear. I am made of fear. Terrified of how severed from myself I've become. Of how utterly impossible it feels that I'll ever find my way into being the one thing I've wanted to be since I was three years old, when my mum taught me to read and I experienced the joy of stories for the first time: *a writer*.

I slip from bed and pad downstairs in the same ugg boots I've had for a decade. Red dirt from my old life still stains their soles.

I make coffee and scuff back upstairs, inhaling my steaming brew. Muted lamplight pools on my writing desk. Icicles cling to the window; the sunrise looks fiery but holds no heat. I add a few drops of Australian eucalyptus oil to my oil burner and light a candle. Three kurkara/desert oak seed pods sitting on a small dish nearby are illuminated in the candlelight. I pick one up and press it into my palm as I flick through the notebook in which I'm writing my first novel by hand, until I find the page where I left off. The sharp edges of the seed pod leave red indents in my skin. I take the cap off my fountain pen. My hands shake. My mind fills with the noise of intrusive thoughts: *I have nothing to write, nothing to say.* The candlewick hisses as it burns. I close my eyes and push the noise aside to hear my memory of the fire popping and hissing in the backyard of the first house I lived in on my own, after I'd moved out of home. The flames reach for the glitter of unfettered desert stars. Beneath my bare feet, the red dirt is warm. Flowering honey grevillea fills the summer night air with heady sweetness. In my memory, I watch and listen to the fire. I am full of joy. I am full of fear.

I open my eyes, back at my desk in Manchester. Through the window, leafless silver birches sway in the cold, milky light. I put the kurkara/desert oak seed pod back on the dish and grip my pen as I re-read the ending of the last scene I wrote and start writing a new sentence, new scene. I write anything that comes to mind. Anything to keep my hand moving. Although anxiety claws at the back of my throat and pounds in my temples, this has become my morning ritual. I do this every day to try to show up for the story I'm writing, and to remember who I was before fear caused me to section off parts of myself. I do this to try to call a long-lost part of myself back to me. To remember how much I love making up and writing stories. To conjure the courage that I feel like I don't have, to tell the story burning me up inside, to remember my life in the desert and bring it back to me, there, in England, a decade and half the world away.

Sitting at my desk and writing, I feel two forces again: joy and fear.

Growing up in the subtropics on Bundjalung Country, on the south-east Queensland coast, my (ill-informed) perception of Australia's desert was that it was eerie and strange, akin to dark woods in northern fairy tales. A place where only dangerous things happened: backpackers were murdered; dingoes stole children; crocodiles lurked, malevolent, until they were brutalised by Crocodile Dundee; and early European desert explorers met their doom. In 1891, 'Where Dead Men Lie', a poem about white men in the desert written by Barcroft Boake, was published in *The Bulletin* magazine. The opening lines are:

Out on the wastes of the Never Never –
That's where the dead men lie!

Mythologising Australia's interior as a place of death, waste and haunting caught on, as did calling it the Never Never.

Thirteen years later, on a December night in London in 1904, a play debuted at the Duke of York's Theatre in London. Written by J.M. Barrie, the play was *Peter Pan*, the story of a boy who could fly. He came from a faraway, fantastical place of wonders and dangers called Never Never Land (which became Neverland when Barrie adapted the play into a book). It's commonly thought that Barrie was inspired by Boake's term for the Australian desert.

It wasn't until I was living on Anangu Country that I began to learn and understand that Australia's desert interior isn't a fantastical, unreal, otherworldly place. It is an ancient, living landscape, holding tens of thousands of years of First Nations stories, knowledge, law, lore and culture, and thriving World Heritage–listed ecologies. As a young white woman, living in the semi-arid desert was a formative experience of my early adulthood. One that cracked me open and began to teach me who I am, as myself, as a descendant of Celtic and Scandinavian settlers on stolen land, and as a human being. I learned that the desert, this place colonialists had termed the 'dead heart' of the continent, was home to an abundance of flora and fauna, and alive with thousands of generations of stories and culture. The landscape was dramatically beautiful, harsh and demanding of respect. I found a home for myself there; living in the desert brought together childhood and teenage parts of me that had been lost, searching for somewhere to belong.

Every day, I marvelled at the dense stands of kurkara/desert oaks, in varying heights and shapes. I'd learned that their deeply furrowed, cork-like bark is fire-retardant. They are slow-growing, straight up and down, skinny in their juvenile years but fast to develop a taproot that can reach subsurface water at depths of over ten metres; once they have that water supply, they mature and form a large, bushy canopy. As Anangu friends told me, these trees get 'fat and happy' with a water source. Many kurkara in the Western Desert are thought to be more than a thousand years old. I will never forget the awe I felt when I learned that they each start as a seed pod, cracked open by fire, which causes them to germinate and grow. But maybe the most personally affecting thing I learned about kurkara is that they are part of the casuarina family. I grew up with she-oaks by the sea. I found strength and courage in that fact: if casuarina trees could adapt to living by ocean or in desert, so could I. I also learned that 100 million years ago, the desert was an inland sea filled with prehistoric marine life; everything there had been shaped by the ancient memory of water. From my house I watched parkilypa/parakeelya, native wildflowers, spring from the earth after rare rainfall, covering the red dirt in fields of pinks, purples, yellows and greens. I learned how to tell the time through the day by the hue of the sand dunes in the light: blazing terracotta, chocolate brown, shadow violet or sometimes moon grey. I came to understand that while visible change to the desert landscape was imperceptible to my eye, creation and destruction co-existed everywhere, happening all the time, inextricable from each other.

The wonder and joy that I felt at being lucky enough to live in such a unique place spilled over into bouts of secret writing. I say secret partially because, at first, I rarely ever talked about my writing and didn't let anyone else read anything I was working on. I remember sitting at my desk on a winter desert morning, with a view of the flowering pukara/thryptomene bushes through my window, as I started writing fragments of a story I called 'The Sea Queen', about a young girl who grew up by the ocean and stopped speaking after the death of her mother, who craved salt and fire, and who one day received a letter with a pressed flower in it from the grandmother she never knew existed. Years later, those story seeds I wrote in the desert became my first novel, *The Lost Flowers of Alice Hart*.

Living in the desert split my life open in the most exhilarating ways I could dream of as a young woman. I loved being there, on Anangu Country. I loved my job and learning and sharing knowledge. I loved the honour and privilege I had of developing a relationship with the landscape, of beginning to learn and know that place.

But gradually life in the desert became a façade. Most of my energy was spent hiding physical and psychological abuse. This kind of violence was not unfamiliar to me. I fell into a cycle of shrinking myself and my behaviour, and keeping up appearances. Eventually I had to acknowledge I was living in mortal fear and was emotionally and geographically isolated with a volatile secret. After living in the desert on and off for four years, I left one morning without farewell or resolution. I was at work one day, but the next day I was gone.

Overnight, I was back in my childhood bedroom in my coastal family home. Red dirt spilled from the torn-apart seams of my life. I recoiled at the sight of it.

In time I noticed I was living with blind spots. I couldn't face any aspect of the brutal, beautiful life I had left behind, or how deeply I missed it. I would not look at photos or go near social media. I was dogged by my grief for the extraordinary desert landscape from which I had uprooted myself, and the slippery after-effects of the violence I had left behind. I was incapacitated by shame and felt forced into a blast zone of fear, loss and grief. I functioned at the most basic level and had nothing left for anything else. Driving two blocks to the shops left me a shaking mess. I didn't have the capacity to accept my circumstances, the totality of my severance from my desert life. That acknowledgement was unfathomable. I was ashamed. It made me vulnerable to what author Sharon Doane calls 'the misconception that women who are abused are weak and passive, perhaps even masochistic or stupid', which also implies 'that the problem lies within the woman'.

In those fledgling months after my life in the desert ended, I reached a stalemate. By only just functioning, I remained in the blast zone. It was a nowhere land, a place where every action I tried to take to move on caused pain, as did every memory, whether pleasant or traumatic, of what I'd left behind.

The first psychologist I met with after I left the desert let me cry. Jane specialised in cognitive behavioural therapy. There was a painting on her wall that I stared at while I turned her box of tissues into papier-mâché.

'Holly, what's your story?' she asked me.

I started to talk about the violence I had experienced.

She shook her head. 'What is *your* story?'

She folded her hands in her lap. 'When you sacrifice what you are made of, when you are cut off from the story that makes you who you are, that's when things break down and go fundamentally wrong.'

I stared at the painting on Jane's wall, at those thick, dark red circles, separated from an empty sky by an ochre line. I was a mere whiff of who I knew myself to be. I was fading and felt severed from my story, from my deepest sense of self. I didn't understand that every choice I had been making in my desert life – what I wore, how I interacted with friends, how I laughed, who I spoke to, where I went, what I talked about, even what I thought – hadn't been authentic self-expression. Hadn't stemmed from a place of creativity or joy. Rather, my behaviour had been carefully constructed from fear, and shaped and modified, in an effort to protect myself. I'd reached a point where I felt made of fear and shame. Every inner story I told myself to make my life easier led to a deeper severance of my self.

I internalised everything, because of shame. As US academic and author Brené Brown says, shame thrives on secret-keeping. I did everything I could to hide what was happening and how I was beginning, as a consequence, to unravel. I was terrified of my own vulnerability. I perceived it as shameful and weak, so developed strategies to avoid feeling vulnerable. I made myself as small as possible. I shrank my feelings and instincts until they could no longer be perceived as a threat. I stayed quiet to keep myself from harm. It was exhausting. The longer I denied myself the truth, the more severely I abandoned myself. Until I reached the point when I left the desert, ultimately exiling myself from the place where, once, I'd flourished and found a true sense of self, and home.

In 1908, four years after *Peter Pan* debuted in London, Jeannie Gunn's autobiographical novel, *We of the Never-Never*, was published. Gunn, the first white woman to settle in the Mataranka area, in Mangarrayi and Yangman Country in the Northern Territory, used fiction to write an account of her experiences. This is from the prelude to the novel:

And All of Us ... in the Land of the Never-Never; in that elusive land with an elusive name – a land of dangers and hardships and privations yet loved as few lands are loved –

a land that bewitches her people with strange spells and mysteries, until they call sweet bitter, and bitter sweet. Called the Never-Never … because they, who have lived in it and loved it Never-Never voluntarily leave it. Sadly enough, there are too many who Never-Never do leave it. Others – the unfitted – will tell you that it is so called because they who succeed in getting out of it swear they will Never-Never return to it. But we who have lived in it, and loved it, and left it, know that our hearts can Never-Never rest away from it.

After I read these words for the first time, they entered my being like red dirt in my uggs: *But we who have lived in it, and loved it, and left it, know that our hearts can Never-Never rest away from it.*

For the past decade, Jeannie Gunn's words have reminded me of my desert life and what that ancient, thriving, living landscape of culture and stories, with its gullies of kurkara/desert oaks, made of me, my life and my unresting heart.

Re-reading Gunn's words now as I write this book, I'm struck by the realisation that creativity is a kind of Never-Never. A vast, rich, extreme landscape we each have inside ourselves. An inner country full of our daydreams, wonders, joys, longings, hopes and pains. A place brimming with the magical quality of infinite possibilities. Somewhere we yearn for, to experience and belong to, to revel in, to love, like any landscape we seek in the natural world. As writer and activist Anne Lamott writes in her book *Stitches: A Handbook on Meaning*, 'A radiance is inside us, just as it is visible outside us, and to seek it is maybe to catch a glimpse from time to time of a light within, of a candle at the window of our heart, of a home somewhere inside.'

I think of the taproot of kurka_ra/desert oaks reaching for water. And what happens if they don't find it. When the radiance inside each of us is neglected, our inner country goes unnourished. When we don't use our creativity, that inner place, brimming with potential, withers. All we see is a desert. All we feel is emptiness. And it haunts us.

This inner country of creativity is one we innately know and frequently inhabit as children. It's an instinctive place we go to when we are young. But as we mature and become adults, many of us begin to forget or entirely lose the way to that inner land. For countless reasons: a figure or situation of power or authority in our lives causes us to doubt ourselves; we develop an inner critic; fear takes hold. In its effort to protect us from a perceived threat, like the vulnerability of creating something, fear convinces us that creativity is a risk. We stop creating. Not creating is safe. One day we might find we can't remember how it feels to create at all. The path to that place of magic and possibility is gone from us. Maybe we've turned our backs on it deliberately. We might have severed ourselves from that place inside and think we've made a clean getaway; we might tell ourselves that the niggle we feel in our hearts, that sense of unrest, is nothing.

But like any natural landscape we love and feel we belong to, that inner country, the place where our imagination resides, will never stop calling for us to return. Unused creativity becomes a burdensome shadow we carry everywhere we go.

When I was a kid, my favourite fairy tales were about other worlds, where I found escapism and comfort. My two favourites were Fantasia from *The Neverending Story* and Neverland in *Peter Pan*. I yearned for my own place in these worlds where I could belong, dream, and feel safe and free. I pined for the magic in those stories to be real, to be awakened one night by a soft tapping at my window and find Falkor the luckdragon from *The Neverending Story* or Peter Pan there at my sill, ready to whisk me away in starlight. (In my teen years, I yearned for Luke Perry to come to my window and magic me into the halls of Beverly Hills High, but that's an altogether different book.) As a child, I wanted to believe in a place I could go to that would allow me to feel joy and teach me how to be resilient and brave and comfortable in my own skin. I remember the euphoria I felt when I realised, with my mum's encouragement, that I could write myself into those worlds I longed for. I filled exercise books with stories and drawings of frightening adventures and joyous homecomings. I learned as a very young child that I could live in two worlds, the one outside myself, and the one within. As writer Anaïs Nin said, writing allowed me 'to taste life twice'.

Decades later, no longer a child, and no longer writing with the ease I'd written with in childhood, there were countless nights after I'd left the desert when I'd take walks and look up at the firmament, secretly imagining a glimpse of a luckdragon's tail or a trail of pixie dust. Wishing I could ignore the unrest in my heart.

In J.M. Barrie's 1911 novel, Peter Pan tells Wendy Darling that the way to Neverland is 'second to the right, and straight on till morning'. It is described as a place 'always more or less an island', though not the same from one child to the next: John Darling's Neverland had 'a lagoon with flamingos flying over it', whereas his brother Michael's Neverland had a 'flamingo with lagoons flying over it'. And children were said to have found the island only because it was 'out looking for them'. It occurs to me now how the directions to Neverland are both specific and elusive, just as directions inwards, to reach the place from which we can allow ourselves to create, can feel. When it comes to expressing our creativity, we know what we need to do and where we want to be, but we don't always know how to get there.

After I left the desert, I moved to a city I'd never lived in before and got a new job. I waited for things to get better, but like the fairy tale in which the princess focuses on acquiring more mattresses instead of addressing the troublesome pea, unresolved trauma haunted me. I lived with a sense of limbo, sunk by a past I wouldn't let myself remember and a future that I couldn't foresee. I was silenced by shame, which kept my secrets unspoken. I couldn't focus on my new job or life. I was restless, forgetful and anxious, and barely coped with menial tasks. My personality had become thin, jittery and ghostly.

Eventually the burden of my secrets became too much. I began meeting with a new psychologist. Let's call her Mary. I wanted to name my ghosts and tell their tales, to be unburdened, to be free. Of course, it wasn't that simple. Although I met regularly with Mary, I grappled with talking about my shame, grief and ghosts. For our first few sessions Mary tried to talk about the effects of post-traumatic stress disorder. 'I'm not that person,' I told her. 'Post-traumatic stress is something experienced by people who have really suffered.'

She looked at me for a long time before she asked about the bright-pink scars on my eyelids. Two months before I'd left the desert, I'd flown to Meanjin/Brisbane and undergone eye surgery to correct chronic stress-induced infections in both eyes. At the time of this discussion with Mary, I had just had the second of what would be three surgeries to eradicate the infections. Acknowledging their cause was something I couldn't face; it became another source of shame and humiliation.

At our next session Mary changed tack and surprised me with a request: 'Tell me about writing.'

I looked at her blankly. Mary reminded me that in our first session together I'd briefly mentioned the stories I'd written when I was a kid. She asked me again. 'Tell me about writing.'

There was lightness in my chest. Slow to start, my answers soon came freely. About the callus I developed on my middle finger as a girl who gripped her pencil too hard and wrote for too long. About the desk that ran the length of my childhood bedroom wall, on whose surface I wrote my stories when I ran out of paper. And about the favourite books I would pack in a bag and take with me when I 'ran away' … to the garden. By sharing those memories, I began telling my ghost story.

'You must write,' Mary said.

My mouth went dry. It had been a long time since I'd written anything.

'No one's going to read it,' she assured me. 'Write the stories inside you, the ones you tell yourself. Start with what you remember, or what you desire. You can write the past. And you can write your future.' Mary leaned forward. 'They are two different things, Holly.' She gave me some journalling exercises to help me get started.

I drove home in a stupor. There was a delicious itch in my fingertips, but an old, loud story dominated my mind. I couldn't write. I had nothing to say. I was no good. My stories were no good. I wasn't smart enough. Talented enough. Strong enough. My imagination was jeopardy, best left alone. That was the story I had been telling myself for years. However, as psychotherapist

Philippa Perry writes, 'We can change a story from one that does not help us to one that does.' And I was about to learn that those inner stories consuming my mind were changeable.

That night, I sat up and wrote until my eyelids were hot and gummy. When I hit a lull, I brewed thick, milky coffee.

By dawn I had written a short story. I experienced not only the rush of having written something whole for the first time in years, but also the strange and cathartic relief of having confronted the ghosts that had been silencing me. Years later, I read the words of Argentinian writer Luisa Valenzuela, who wrote that anything that goes unsaid acquires the importance of a scream. I had a long-silenced scream in my soul, and by taking that first step and writing that story, I had found my voice. Through my creativity – writing – I screamed at the top of my lungs. It was a painful, blissful alchemy. In that single act of writing, I had, for just one night, changed an old inner story that had oppressed me into a new one that liberated me: I'd given myself permission to write. I had allowed myself to be the kid who loved to make up stories and lose herself in writing them.

What I couldn't have known then was that by writing a short story through the night, until the magpies started warbling at dawn, I'd set my life on a new trajectory. A seed had split open in the dirt of my inner country, twitching with new beginnings.

I stayed in therapy. I kept writing. I saved every dollar I could from my paycheques. I wobbled and stumbled through my new life. The sense of limbo persisted. I knew I couldn't stay where I was.

With the support I found in therapy and with a few trusted friends, I started to let myself remember the neglected dreams hidden inside me. They weren't lifeless and ashen. They were glowing embers. Alight. Waiting.

A year later, I moved alone to the UK. Where I'd never been before and knew no one, and where I'd applied for and been offered a place on a Master of Arts in Creative Writing course at the University of Manchester. I was in the privileged position of being able to use my life savings to travel from Australia to the other side of the world and study the art form I loved most at tertiary level. I hadn't applied for a place on the MA because I believed that studying writing at university would make me the writer I yearned to be. I'd applied because moving to the other side of the world felt like it was the only way I could try to rebuild my life from the ground up. But I was terrified to go out alone into the world. To have no sense of the city or country I'd moved to. No friends or family. No memories, even though that was also the allure. Knowing that in England my life would be oriented around writing, not vice versa, was the safety net I needed. It gave me a sense of identity, purpose, meaning and validation that I clung to. I moved to Manchester to study writing because I needed to know I was moving towards something, towards myself, rather than the opposite.

It took another five years of living overseas, being in therapy, pushing my way through the mud of post-traumatic stress patterns, before I had a cataclysmic reckoning with myself. I'd graduated with my MA. I was writing. Engaging my creativity, I thought. Tending my inner country, I thought. But I couldn't understand why my imagination still felt blocked. Why I still felt so brittle with fear. Why my writing felt arid and thirsty rather than luscious and joyous as I remembered it could feel. I was tormented and anguished, wondering what more I could do. I felt strangled by the intrusive thoughts of my inner critic and swallowed whole by vast forms of fear.

The tipping point came in 2014, when I sat in hospital beside someone in my family as they died. It was a devastating, transformative experience. The wild, maddening grief and shock. The overwhelming love and sorrow. The profundity of bearing witness as they took their last breath. And hearing the quiet when their next breath didn't come. Until then, I'd never been with any being I loved when they died. Neither a human nor an animal.

The full impact of experiencing the end of life sent an earthquake through me. I was, quite mercilessly, shaken from the vice that had been choking my mind: in that hospital room, I realised exactly what fear does to us when it's the source of our actions and beliefs. How it shrinks us and reduces us and robs us of fully living our lives. Fear, I understood with brutal clarity, is suffering little deaths constantly inside ourselves: choices we could bring to life by saying yes to but that we say no to instead. Because possibility, for countless reasons, frightens us. So we keep ourselves closed and bound. That's what we perceive to be the safest option. How wrong we are, I remember thinking that day as my family and I sat with our beloved's body in hospital. How dangerous is unchecked fear when it's driving our decision-making. What a thief it is, robbing us of our very own lives.

For the first few sluggish weeks of bereavement, I found myself in quiet moments turning to books and writings about creativity. I couldn't read another grief pamphlet, I couldn't concentrate or focus for long enough to read fiction or anything else. But I did seem able to read about creativity and imagination. I found it to be the only subject that soothed me. I had no idea what was about to happen to my life.

About a month later, I was at home alone when a particularly tempestuous wave of grief sent me to my writing desk. I was buoyed by it, and sick of feeling pinned down by fear, decades of fear. In a rage, I rummaged through my desk for a notebook and pen.

'What would happen?' I demanded of myself aloud, 'if for once I didn't listen to the fears in my head that I've been listening to for as long as I can remember? What if fear wasn't the first thing I listened to?'

I opened my notebook and took the lid off my pen as I bargained with myself.

'What if I *didn't* listen to all the reasons I can't do this?'

The next moment is one I will treasure and revere for the rest of my life.

As though I was outside my body, I watched my hand write the first words that came into the tiny quiet space I'd carved out in my mind, no matter how many fearful thoughts were pressing in from all sides: 'In the weatherboard house at the end of the lane, nine-year-old Alice Hart sat at her desk by the window and dreamed of ways to set her father on fire.'

I sat back and dropped my pen. I remember saying something aloud like, 'Holy fuck,' followed by, 'Here she is.'

And there she was. Alice Hart, the main character of my debut novel. Suddenly, in that moment, I found myself obliged to a nine-year-old child who needed me to tell her story. I knew, looking at the words I'd written by hand on my page, that despite how my hands were shaking, I would not let fear stop me showing up for her.

And now.

Fifteen years after I left the desert.

Fourteen years after I moved to England.

Nine years after that moment writing by hand at my desk.

I am here on a clear-dawning morning on Bundjalung Country, southeast Queensland, by the sea. I've been woken by vivid golden light. It's 2023. I'm forty-two years old, an author of two novels, and I'm writing my third book. This one. About joy, and fear and creativity.

I'm here because of the kid I was who knew the power and joy of writing from her inner country to her outer page. I'm here because of the woman I was who didn't know the difference between protecting herself and abandoning herself. And because of the woman I was in 2014, writing in the cold light of dawn with red dirt still in her ugg boots and ink stains on her fingers, shaking with the effort it took to muster the courage to write the story and place she loved and longed for inside herself. I'm also here because of years of seeking help and support, both professional and personal. I am all those women. All those experiences. All those landscapes.

I go into the kitchen and flick the kettle on to boil. Watch the pastel sky change over the ocean. I take my coffee into my office. Light one candle, say a quiet prayer of thanks to be writing on this land, and refill my fountain pens with ink. I consider why I practise these rituals and it feels mostly like they are a process akin to taking your shoes off before you enter a temple. I have learned that these are my preparations and prayers before I immerse myself in a space that is sacred. The inner country. Deeply human, timeless, connected, unknown, frightening, magical and essential. The source that Carl Jung described when he asked, 'What did you do as a child that made the hours pass like minutes? Herein lies the key to your earthly pursuits.'

I open my notebook. My hand quivers.

I still feel them both in my body, right now, simultaneously, as I write this prologue: joy and fear. Both jostling. Both surging. I still have to manage which of these two forces will guide and shape what I bring from the country inside me to the land of my page.

Truth: if my creativity, my interior country, built of my wildest dreams and brimming with dangers and wonders, is my own Never-Never, and I have lived in it and loved it and left it – for whatever reason – I will never, never rest away from it.

Truth: at any age, at any time, we can decide anew to return to the home of creativity inside ourselves. We can find the courage to cultivate that inner country, to nurture it, to grow and build a space inside for the joy it brings us. I did it. So can you. Imagination is something every single one of us has, made of everything that makes us who we are: courage, grief, vulnerability, shame, hope, love … No matter how we abandon it, how old we grow, or how far away from ourselves we've drifted, our courage to create, despite all the things that have stopped us, is there. Here. In me. And you. Imagine your dream house, a space where you are always welcome. A light always left on for you to come home to.

Truth: it can be frightening to return to our inner country of creativity and to dare to nurture and build a place for ourselves there. At the core of so many of us is a deep craving for directions that will allow us to go back to that creative place inside. It took me years of sitting at my desk and writing by hand to find the courage to realise that the directions I needed were hidden inside a choice. Choosing the grace of giving myself permission to write was the light left on, a glow in the dark guiding my way, a glow that shame, fear and self-doubt, though they pressed in on me, could not dim.

Truth: the choice to create because we love to do it is ours. The inner country of creativity and the house we build there are ours.

Truth: it's always fearful. Always joyful.

A light is always left on. Always guiding. Always waiting for us to arrive.

Welcome.

Truth: at any age, at any time, we can decide anew to return to the home of creativity inside ourselves.

Our House

Do you remember the first time someone told you to hold a seashell up to your ear and listen? And, as you listened, they asked something like, *Can you hear the ocean?*

The first time I remember this happening to me, I was about four years old, visiting my beloved grandmother. The memory of hearing the ocean through the shell Granny had pressed against my ear, despite her house being far from the sea, still fills me with a shiver of awe. The joy I find in this memory comes from two separate thoughts: remembering the excitement that I felt as a kid, our capacity for wonder in childhood; and learning what's actually happening when we hold a seashell to our ear. The shell functions as a kind of resonance chamber, capturing ambient noise that is already all around us and bouncing that noise around inside the shell. This creates the sound we hear, when the shell is pressed to our ear, as the crashing waves of the ocean.

My hope for this book is that it can be a seashell to your ear ... maybe a little bit magical, maybe a little bit wonderful, but mostly bringing to your attention what's already right here, there, in you and around you, waiting for you to notice.

Sometimes when I'm writing, I like to think about what is at the heart of my work. At the heart of this book is a question:

Why should I create?

The answers are as vast as an ocean. Universal and individual. Simply put, creativity is present, whether we engage with it or not, in every aspect of ourselves and our lives. It's an innate part of being human. We know this as children, and often slowly forget this as we age. Nevertheless, we're creating even when we don't think we are. Even if we say we're not 'creative', our very beings are animated by creativity. Within varying means, constraints and privileges, creativity is present within us every day of our lives – from how we visually and audibly express ourselves, to how we spend our spare time, show people we love them or choose what to make for a meal, to how we decorate our homes, pick gifts to give to others or even select background wallpapers for our phones. The function of our imagination is often not conscious to us. Creativity is also all around us. In the architecture of the world, the music we listen to, the books we read, the games we play, the advertising vying for our attention everywhere, the series we stream on TV, the movies we see, the art we absorb in galleries and through social media, the memes, the videos. Creativity is an outer landscape we walk through every day, as well as an inner country of our own private making.

The simplest answer to my question is that we create because it's human. When we do it consciously it's usually because we want to. Creating makes us feel good. Brings us a sense of mindfulness. Makes hours pass like minutes. Creativity enriches our lives. It is, as writer and performer Kae Tempest says, 'the ability to feel wonder and the desire to respond to what we find startling'. It is 'any act of love,' says Tempest, and that could include anything from choosing clothes to raising children to devoting your time and attention to a loved one.

When we create and feel joy, we stir up creative inspiration in other people. Like courage, and fear, creativity is contagious. As writer and activist Maya Angelou said, 'You can't use up creativity. The more you use, the more you have.' To create is something we are born with a capacity and instinct to do – avoiding creativity because of fear, guilt or shame is something we learn.

This book is an offering to anyone, and their inner country of creative calling, at any stage of development and engagement. It's for writers, but it's also for gardeners, carpenters, sculptors, jewellery-makers, yoga teachers, fashion designers, florists, songwriters, dancers, cooks, painters … anyone with a desire to create but who, like me, sometimes stumbles to engage with that desire because of fear. Fear of feeling afraid, of vulnerability, of criticism and judgement from others, of shame, of facing the past, of facing ourselves, of not being good enough, of not having enough, of having 'bad' ideas, of having 'good' ideas, of being 'too much'. That is who this book is for – those who are stuck creatively, who long to create but don't know how to find a way into, or back to, their imagination.

Elizabeth Gilbert, author of *Big Magic*, wrote that we should create whatever causes a revolution in our heart. If you've been looking for an invitation to turn the key and unlock a revolution in your heart, please consider that this book might be it. Please come back here if you need a reminder that creativity brings you joy, that you are allowed to create and to feel joy, and that you are brave enough to answer creativity when it calls to you. In the words of comedian, actor and writer Tina Fey, 'Say yes and you'll figure it out afterwards.' Revel in your imagination for the pure joy of it. It's only human of you. The pleasure we experience when we create is the reason to do it and is the way into ourselves.

As I type these words, I'm sitting at my desk with honey myrtle essential oil burning in my diffuser, looking through the window at a blue autumn sky. Near me is the bouquet of pale pink and green Asiatic lilies I bought to have within view while I'm writing. As I work at my keyboard, the petals jiggle and shake from the vibrations of my typing. It's often too hard/fraught/terrifying to let myself think about, but in this moment I understand that these words are travelling as thoughts from my brain and body, through my fingertips, to this document on my screen, which will soon travel far from me to eventually emerge as printed ink marks on paper. Paper that began as a seed, in earth, then split open to grow over years into a tree, and was eventually bound with a beautiful cover, and will be packed into a box then unpacked onto a bookshelf, and, finally ... be with you. Wherever you are, in geography, in life, you're holding this book between your hands and reading these words right now, taking them into your mind and body. We're working some kind of human magic, me, these words and you.

What an extraordinary thing.

If this book is a seed pod, the generosity and kindness of reader responses to my work are the fire that first set it ablaze and cracked it open. Since 2018, meeting and communing with readers on my book tours and online, hearing their stories and their questions about creativity, I slowly began to realise two things: we are never as alone in our strangeness as we think we are, and we are often so much braver than we think.

The first seed sprouted in October 2022. I was on tour with my second novel, *The Seven Skins of Esther Wilding*, and was meeting readers during my book signing after an event in Boorloo/Perth. Two of them were Natalia and Sherron.

While I was signing their books, Natalia quietly asked me a question. 'How do you allow yourself to make art? Why should we bother creating anything at all when the world is burning?'

Natalia's question hit me square in the chest. I took a deep steadying breath before I spoke. 'Because it's what we have to offer each other,' I heard myself say.

Giving ourselves permission to create and to revel in the joy of creating is a powerful act of resisting cynicism and scarcity. To choose to make art when there's so much grief, despair, suffering, cruelty and tragedy in the world is to choose to connect with the best parts of ourselves and each other as humans. To connect with our ability to create beauty. Beauty fuels us to widen our minds, to be open-hearted and curious, and to rage against becoming apathetic. To resist living in fear. To welcome joy. As writer Maria Dahvana Headley said in her 2023 Tolkien Lecture, 'If you stop imagining things other than your own self and your own experience, you end up really stuck and also really afraid.'

When we choose to create in the face of fear, we inspire others to choose their own creativity over fear too. Giving ourselves permission to answer what calls to our hearts creates an energy that catches. Like fire. As author, coach and activist Karen Walrond says, 'I will never apologise for embracing joy and beauty – even when the world is falling apart – because joy and beauty are my fuel for activism.'

For months after meeting Natalia and Sherron that night, I thought about our conversation. I didn't know I had that answer about creativity until I spoke with them. Another gift that readers have given me.

Before I tell you more about what this book is, it's important to say what it's not. This isn't a how-to book. Neither is it a workbook full of exercises. It's not a step-by-step guide to creative writing, or writing a novel, or being a 'good' writer, or becoming any other kind of artist. It is not written by a neurological, behavioural or social science expert.

This book doesn't assume that we have the same circumstances, come from the same childhoods or backgrounds, or have equal privilege and opportunities. It doesn't assert that creativity is above, separate from or more important than social justice, racial and cultural equality, employment, housing, food, education and funding for arts programs in all communities. When talking about the power of choice we have as artists, this book doesn't suggest that gross systemic dysfunction and societal oppression are issues from which any individual can free themselves by choice.

I'm not a qualified therapist, psychologist, psychiatrist or counsellor. Reading about fear, grief, joy, shame, vulnerability, trauma and recovery may be triggering for some people. If this is the case for you, please go gently. Seek the professional help, assessment and support you need if reading this book brings up any issues for you – details for helplines are included in the end pages.

This book *is* a series of connected essays that share my experience of acknowledging and understanding how fear in its varying forms blocked my creativity and stopped me for many years from writing the stories knocking at my chest, begging to be told, since I was a kid. This book is about how I've learned to tap into my creativity and write from my inner country, that place of magic and possibility, despite feeling deep terror about doing so. And how the power of allowing myself to do the thing I love, the singular thing I've known about myself all my life, has blown up many of the ways I'd kept myself small for much of my adult life.

Learning how to let myself write because it's what I love to do has never meant that I'm not fearful while I'm writing. It means that through writing I also feel joy equal to and greater than the fear that stopped me for all those years. Giving myself permission to write, to create, has changed the way I live. I'm sharing these reflections and notes on creativity in the hope that they will be of value or meaning to anyone who thinks they are alone in experiencing the chokehold of fear every time they dare to try to answer the creative calling knocking in their chests.

In the chapters that follow, I explore eight types of fear-based experiences that I'm confronted with every time I write. (The fears I experience are far from being limited to eight types, but none of us wants this book to rival *War and Peace* in its length.) I respond to each of these experiences with actions or states of mind, and describe how I practise them so that I can continue to give myself permission to create and feel joy. Combined, these make what I call my Toolkit of Unfuckable-with Magic, TUM for short, which I love because unfuckable-with magic does tend to come from gut instinct.

What's in my TUM may not be the same as what's in yours. Your TUM could be full of different tools. Sharing my tools and processes is an offering. Take or leave anything that doesn't resonate. As I said, this is not a how-to book. This is not dictation. Fear and joy, like grief, like love and hope and shame and courage, are universal. And individual. What has been and is my experience might not be yours. None of this is prescriptive.

Toolkit of Unfuckable-with Magic (TUM)

WHEN I FEEL:	I MEET IT WITH:
FEAR	PLAY
SELF-DOUBT	SELF-COMPASSION
FAILURE	'NOTHING IS WASTED'
PROCRASTINATION	PRESENCE
INNER CRITICISM	MY INNER FAN
OUTER CRITICISM	RESILIENCE
CREATIVELY BLOCKED	MY DAYDREAM MACHINE
IMPOSTER SYNDROME	'I BELONG HERE'

At the end of each chapter, you'll find Provocations. These are questions for your reflection. There are no right or wrong answers, just *your* answers. You might want to answer them like a rapid-fire quiz, to avoid overthinking and get your gut response. Or you might want to take them slowly and ponder which answer feels truest to you. Consider these Provocations as doorways you can open and go through to see what's on the other side. Maybe you'll find something unexpected or long forgotten. Maybe you'll surprise yourself.

In the context of these pages, an artist isn't defined by whether they derive money from their creativity. When I use the word 'artist' in this book, I'm describing anyone engaged in creative thinking and the creative process.

When I write about joy in this book, I'm not only referring to the kind of joy that feels good, euphoric, ecstatic, happy. They are deeply pleasurable types of joy to experience and ones I live for. I'm also talking about the joy that floods us, that hurts in its poignancy, that moves us to tears. The joy of feeling purpose and meaning. The joy of connection. The joy of being understood, of feeling seen, of feeling like we belong. The joy of safety and community. The joy of bearing witness, of staying open when we want to shut down, the joy of remaining curious, of sharing grief, of encouraging change and transformation in ourselves and each other. The joy of naming what shames us, and the joy of believing we're still, in all our imperfections, loveable. I'm talking about the joy of feeling. Not numbing.

I turn to the poets. I read Audre Lorde, who talks of the importance of sharing joy so that it lessens the difference between us. I read Ross Gay, who writes about the necessary entangling of joy with pain and suffering and sorrow. And finally, I read Toi Derricotte, whose poem 'Joy is an Act of Resistance' gives me a mantra for life and work.

Opening myself to joy in all its facets is how I become the evolving human (and writer) that I am. As we all are. It's not always comfortable, it's not always pleasurable, it's not always easy, and I feel like I stumble more than I glide. But I'm no longer hidden away by shame. Stories that I couldn't speak for so many years no longer silence me. I have found ways to write, despite being terrified. I'm still terrified. I'm still writing. It's an ongoing practice.

The title of this book came to me before I could fully understand what the book itself would be. I was putting away washing, thinking about writing and joy, which reminded me of my favourite Mary Oliver poem, 'We Shake With Joy'. In just four lines, Mary Oliver describes joy and grief as being irrevocably entwined. Reading her acknowledgement of this – that joy and grief are indivisible – had a profound effect on me. Thinking of joy and grief living together, inseparable from one another, prompted me to imagine a house. Inside myself. In the inner country of my dreams, where everything is possible, magical, sacred, tender and treasured, I imagined this house, a place of safety and nourishment for my imagination and creativity. It was a house built of hard-fought joy. And, I understood then, a house built of joy inside me was also a house that would give grief a home.

A sentence I have never imagined I would write, let alone publish: the whole truth about the title of this book is that it was inspired by both Mary Oliver and … American football. The last place that I, a non-team-sports-following-writer-person, would ever have thought I would find seminal inspiration and guidance for life as an author was in a football chant. But here we are.

I first heard the rallying cry 'Whose House? Our house!' in an episode of the beloved television series *Friday Night Lights*. Inspired by the real chant used by a Texas university, it's shouted in the series by high school football players before a game to motivate themselves and to remember to play with honour and integrity, not dirty tricks.

At the time I first heard the chant I was emotionally porous, in ripe condition to be affected by something as random as an American football chant. *The Lost Flowers of Alice Hart* had been published, I'd been touring it and talking publicly about hard, true, beautiful things, constantly walking the line between reliving and reflecting on traumatic memories so that I could authentically share the background story of writing the novel. But talking day after day about my past experiences living with violence took a toll. I felt skinless and unsteady. The therapist I was seeing at the time implored me to rest, warning of things like burnout and post-traumatic-stress flare-ups. I was in England, which very helpfully meant I had ample rainy days at my disposal to spend on my couch. Flicking through streaming services looking for something comforting to watch, I found and binged *Friday Night Lights*. For the next few months, I stomped around my house ranting and chanting little else. 'Whose house? Our house!'

It became my cry of defiance, mantra-like, as I recovered my strength. It reminded me of what I would accept in my life, my heart and my inner country, and how important it was to protect my creativity, my capacity to stay open and curious, and my ability to believe in the good in myself and other people and to set healthy boundaries. Whose house? Mine. My imaginary house. My inner country. My space, my safety, my creativity. Where I could choose who and what I allowed to come inside. My life. My mind.

A television show about American high school football players reminded me I was my own protector, and I could be emotionally open, strong, resilient, joyful, vulnerable and true all at once.

Joy and grief.

Living together. Under one roof.

One house.

Our House

The one we build for our hearts on the inner country of our lives, that's made of joy and gives home to grief. Where we're always welcome. Where we always belong. Where we can always return, to nurture and replenish and create.

Whose house?
Our house.

When I talk in personal experience terms in this book about creativity, unless I'm specific, I'm always talking about writing. I express myself creatively in many other ways too, but writing is my source. Yours might be different. From making model trains to surfing, from collecting rocks to playing the piano, from designing shoes to collecting stamps, we all have different sources of creativity.

But this is how creativity – writing – happens for me.

I sit at my desk and remind myself I'm there because underneath everything else – fear, self-doubt, anxiety – writing is joy. It is noticing. It is feeling. It is connecting. It is imagining. It is being human, reduced to sentences, word by word making the bones and flesh and skin of story. Stories are alive. They breathe and grow as we do. They nourish and guide us, blind and free us.

Sometimes, very rarely, writing is glamorous. I'll shower and dress up for my desk. Wear favourite earrings or a talisman around my neck. Other times, like today, it's just however I turn up. As long as I do.

The main thing is unwavering in its sameness: turn up. I remind myself of this all the time.

Turn up for who you were when you didn't know how to find courage to try but kept dreaming. Turn up for the stories and ideas that need you to bring them to life.

I remind myself: everything you want in your soul only has a chance of becoming if you turn up. Summon the conviction to get out of your own way and let your imagination lead you.

It's not word counts or ticked-off scenes.

It's not page numbers or plotlines.

They come later.

Before anything else, writing is turning up. Creativity is turning up. Because you want to. Because it brings you joy. Because it's what you love. It's the wonder of choosing to commit to something bigger than and beyond you.

How beautiful an act, to have faith in yourself as you make something from nothing. Whatever it is that sets your heart on fire, whether it's playing the trumpet or sketching clouds, turn up.

Turn up.

Turn.

Up.

First one word, then another.

I remind myself.

Everything you want in your soul only has a chance of becoming if you turn up.

Some of the 'what-ifs' going through my mind as I write this book:

What if I have nothing to say?

What if the book is shit?

What if people are mean about the book and me on the internet?

What if I can't do it?

What if people hate it? Hate me?

What if everyone misunderstands the book and me and I make a total dick of myself?

We all have these inner dialogues. But:

What if it surprises me? What if I unearth something beautiful that I'm not aware of?

What if writing this book teaches me things that I can't imagine I don't know?

What if I can do it?

What if I can?

What if writing this book is building a new house on my inner country? For the joy of being an author? For the joy of having readers? For the joy of the connection and magic between my words becoming yours?

What if I can?

What if you feel like you can too?

Our House

What if the music of the ocean is already in us and around us?
    What if we really don't need a shell to hear it?
What if the only opinion worth listening to when we need guidance
    is our own?
What if our house is our house?
What if we can protect our magic?
What if we're braver than we think?
What if everything we need to create is already in us?
What if you can?
What if I can?
What if we can?

We can.

1

Fear + Play: Raise Your Sword

The house I grew up in had floor-to-ceiling bay windows in the lounge room. They looked out into my mum's garden, which, during the day, made them tranquil portals of green beauty. But at night, when it grew dark outside and we had the inside lights on, the windows became black, opaque and reflective. More than that: to my young mind, they were rectangles of darkness and fear. Even though I was a kid, I had enough awareness to understand that through the windows I was visible to the outside world, but the outside world wasn't visible to me. It was my first experience of understanding that just because I couldn't see something I feared didn't mean that it didn't exist. Here, now as I type, I can still feel the sensation in my body. How, when I stood in front of those windows, my little body grew heavy with the weight of a cold flood of fear.

When I started writing my first novel, I struggled to understand and articulate the fear I was feeling about sharing my work. This was before I had a publisher, or an agent. This was when I was terrified of letting anyone read my writing. My fear of being read, the cold flood of it, was so familiar, but I couldn't grasp why.

That changed on a grey London afternoon in 2015. I was sitting in a bright café with beloved friend and author Brooke Davis. We were talking about the vulnerability of sharing our work. I hadn't thought about those windows in my childhood home in decades, and yet I heard myself telling Brooke about them in vivid detail. There I was, maybe six years old, freshly bathed, in my pjs, in the lounge room, trying to focus on watching television and not on looking at the black windows beside me. (Eventually I told my mum about how much the windows frightened me, but not even drawing the thin calico curtains could satisfy me. The windows were still visible. As was the darkness. As was everything I could not see.)

Brooke asked me if I'd grown out of the fear, or if something had happened to make it lose its hold on me. Her insightful question prompted me to go deeper into the memory. After getting fed up with feeling so frightened of the windows every

Holly, in her She-Ra headpiece with sword and cuffs, and her mother, Colleen

time I wanted to sit in my beanbag and watch TV, the night eventually came when I hatched a plan. I emerged from my bedroom brandishing the gold plastic She-Ra sword Mum had bought me in a show bag from the Ekka – the Brisbane Royal Agricultural Show. (I was also wearing the matching gold plastic She-Ra headpiece and cuffs that were included in said show bag too.) Striding into the lounge room, I raised my sword and hissed at the windows. Satisfied that I had vanquished the darkness, the unseen watchers, the ghosts, I sat in my beanbag with my sword at my side and my headpiece firmly in place while I enjoyed an hour of Sunday-night Disney. After that, I don't remember fearing the dark windows in the same way.

I notice that as I'm writing this now, my hands are clammy. My stomach is in knots. The fear of being seen, of being vulnerable to unknown judgement, has not lost its hold. But to remember that kid with her sword and crown, hissing into the void of darkness, embodying with her whole spirit the kind of courage she wanted to possess, I'm reminded that if I've got anywhere with meeting and managing fear in my life, it's been through remembering and embracing the power of play.

While I was working with Mary, the psychologist I met with after I left the desert, we spent a session exploring four common stress responses to fear: fight, flight, freeze and fawn.

As explained by psychotherapist Astrid Burke in relation to Pete Walker's book *Complex PTSD: From Surviving to Thriving*, the *fight* response is about protecting and preserving ourselves by engaging in conflict – we might get a mad burst of adrenaline, we might pick fights with others, we might deflect by seeking control through defensiveness. *Flight*, by contrast, is about seeking to prevent pain through escape. We hide in bathrooms at parties, avoid difficult conversations or ghost people on the phone. We worry, panic and micromanage, so much so that people in flight response might seem obsessed with work or study or with doing things perfectly. The *freeze* response is when we seek protection through dissociation. We feel paralysed by stress, cut ourselves off from others, find it difficult to make or follow through on decisions, and become passive, sticking to our routines and making no new plans. *Fawn* is, in contrast to fight, a response whereby we seek to protect ourselves by placating others. When we're in fawn, we're people-pleasers, appeasing others through flattery, never saying no, putting our own needs last, and constantly thinking about what others need or want so as to be useful or valuable to them.

In one of our earliest sessions, Mary asked me if I identified with any of the four stress responses. I replied with a snort of misplaced laughter. Mary waited for me to gather myself. I told the truth: I'd felt all four stress responses in situations when I'd been in physical and psychological danger.

As I write this, I pause to think about the ways I know fear in my mind and body. A pounding head and heart. Churning stomach. Heavy limbs. Cold sweats. The shakes. Blurry vision. Fidgeting. Nausea. A forced smile. Unsteady, shallow breathing. I think back to that session with Mary and I remember it wasn't just affecting because I started to understand how fear plays out in our behaviour when we're confronted by a dangerous situation. It was also affecting because I realised that I'd experienced stress responses not only when I was in real danger, but also when I was in what I wrongly perceived as a threatening situation. Like wanting to create, to write. I didn't seem able to tell the difference between the threat of real danger and a perceived threat from my creativity, that my writing was dangerous. Because to write was to go inside, to remember, to feel. It was vulnerable and unknown. And being vulnerable and facing the unknown was unsafe and to be avoided. So I didn't create. I didn't write.

Later in our fateful session together, when Mary encouraged me to write and sent me home with journalling exercises, there was a spark in my mind. I'd been given a writing task. And writing to me meant creativity. At that point, creativity was an abandoned house with a neglected overgrown garden in the dark woods of my inner country, towards which I hadn't ventured in a long time. I got home from the session and read the exercise: *Describe a time when you have felt afraid and overcome that fear.* I felt my spine shrivel in repulsion.

I was at odds with myself. Flint had been struck, I felt the spark inside me at the thought of writing … but the exercises Mary had given me caused me to shut down, not open up. Journalling asked me to face my vulnerabilities and fears directly – things I was desperate to deny, separate myself from and escape. I'm pretty sure I threw the exercises in the bin. Instinctively, I knew: the only way I could write, despite the fear that stopped me from writing, was by tapping into my memory of myself as that kid with her exercise books filled with handwritten stories. By remembering how it felt to sit at my desk as a girl, writing freely, creating story worlds that I revelled in with untold joy. I learned that night, after my session with Mary, that creating and writing stories I loved was my grown equivalent of putting on the She-Ra headpiece, raising my golden plastic sword and hissing at both my reflection in the glass and the darkness beyond the window. That was the night I sat and wrote until dawn, when I had a short story, a whole short story, on paper. The thing I'd allowed myself to create was the first fiction I'd written in years. Something in that long-neglected garden on my inner country bloomed.

As my sessions with Mary continued, I kept writing. Creating. Vignettes, short stories, flash fiction. Writing creatively became the source of play in my life. It enabled me to draw out my inner narratives, to write past experiences into other story skins, which offered me protection from confronting memories that were too traumatic and harmful to access or recall directly. Through my creativity, writing fiction became an act of play, an act of conjuring shame, secrets and vulnerabilities. I needed to conjure stories that didn't feel autobiographical. I needed to conjure my vulnerabilities and secrets without acknowledging them as such. For the kind of self-expression I craved, I needed to subvert the fear that was keeping me in limbo. I needed to continue to reconnect with a version of myself beneath and separate from years of compounded fears.

Conjuring deep emotional truths through writing fiction enabled me to do this: the women in my stories weren't me. I wrote them as characters I could approach sideways. Writing fiction allowed me to engage with memory but from a distance, a curious, playful distance, where I was able to occupy the lives of the women I wrote about and yet feel separate from them. Through writing, I could empathise with their circumstances, explore their feelings, notice their actions without judgement, and witness their challenges without being accountable for them. Under the guise of fiction, I was able to draw out my inner narratives and confess my vulnerabilities without censoring myself, without being obstructed by shame, secrecy or fear. It was subconscious; I was compelled to write as an Other as a way of distinguishing myself from who I was at that time, from who I was expressing from my past.

Unable to assess, consider or evaluate my experiences in the desert, the only way I began to recover my memories was through writing. Fiction allowed me to begin the process of separating myself from damaging, fearful experiences, to make characters of the emotions that had been controlling me: grief, fear, anxiety, stress. Fiction enabled me to freely express my emotional truth.

Writing myself into a fictional Other was a method of objectifying myself to regain some measure of control over my life after feeling I had none. Through the play of make-believe and writing fiction, I was able to take agency of my life, and give myself the joy of creating.

As my sessions with Mary continued, she talked often with me about fear as a feeling, an innate human response to danger. She told me that we are born with two fears: fear of falling, and fear of loud noises. The rest of our fears are learned, in innumerable ways for innumerable reasons. Maybe we saw a parent or guardian react with fear to a situation, or maybe we were repeatedly told and taught that a situation, scenario, feeling, place or person was to be feared. Mary explained that there were ways to teach ourselves how not to fear things we've perceived as a threat. Like the way I'd found writing fiction to be a playful act that brought me pleasure, which taught me that writing wasn't to be feared in the way I'd been so scared of it previously.

Driving home after one of our sessions, I replayed some of our conversations in my mind. By the time I got back to my share house, I was jittery with emotion. It took me a while, pacing around my bedroom, to realise that I was feeling a mixture of nerves, excitement and possibility. I kept pacing as I connected the dots: if I had learned to feel afraid, maybe I could learn to feel safe.

Breakthrough

My bedroom in that share house had a weird small adjoining room that had no fixtures. Since I'd moved in, I'd done nothing with it and it had remained empty. That night, my pacing took me from my bedroom into the small empty room. I switched the light on. Stood in the middle of the room, glanced at my reflection in the window. The dark beyond. I looked around the room. Until that point, the fiction I'd been writing had been done in my bed, on the couch, in the bath, in the back garden. I started pacing again. If I could learn to feel afraid, maybe I could learn to feel safe in situations and spaces that scared me. Maybe I could learn to cultivate that space, to decorate it and create a place where I felt safe, to make it playful, pleasurable and powerful. Maybe I could make a place for writing stories that felt wonderful to occupy. I recalled painter Georgia O'Keeffe's words to inspire some grit and courage: 'I've always been absolutely terrified every single moment of my life, and I've never let it stop me from doing a single thing I wanted to do.'

Standing in that empty room I decided it would become my writing office. And it would become a place and source of joy.

On my run this morning alongside the Pacific Ocean, I watched surfers of all ages and abilities running down the sand with surfboards at their sides, then paddling out to meet the swell. As

I ran, I thought about all the different forms of play we seek, the vital importance of making space for play in our lives, and all the reasons we don't. One of the most stubbornly persistent is that play is only for children and should only happen in a sandpit or playground or preschool.

When I got home from my run with all these thoughts swirling in my mind, I took a plain question to the fount of (scrutable) wisdom in our digital age: what is play?

Google, by way of Wikipedia, told me, 'Play is a range of intrinsically motivated activities done for recreational pleasure and enjoyment. Play is commonly associated with children and juvenile-level activities, but may be engaged in at any life stage, and among other higher-functioning animals as well, most notably mammals and birds.'

The delight I felt after reading that last sentence sent me further down an internet rabbit hole. In 2009, author and ethologist (someone engaged in the scientific study of animal behaviour) Jonathan Balcombe published the findings of an extensive survey of animals, pleasure and play, which had determined that animals seek and experience happiness for happiness's sake. Herring gulls, for example, were observed playing 'drop-catch' with clams and other like-sized objects as though they were balls, just for fun. Another study, from the University of Tennessee, reported that a male Cuban crocodile was observed allowing a smaller female crocodile to climb onto his back before giving her rides around their pool.

A BBC Earth report on play in animals stated that ravens have been observed 'snowboarding' down frozen roofs and, once they reached the bottom, starting the process all over again. The same article detailed young elephants using riverside embankments as waterslides.

Then there are, of course, the examples of play, pleasure-seeking and joy in animals we know and witness up close – our pets. As a woman who lives with a pack of dogs, I'm confident when I say that I know no other being on Earth more attuned to their need for pleasure and joy than Poppy, one of our said pack, who comes in promptly at four o'clock every afternoon to bark and headbutt the front door to let us know it's time to play ball. Then she runs and chases the ball until she collapses, and, I will maintain, grins for the duration.

After about two hours of reading about animal joy, I came across some thoughts on this topic from Irene Lobato Vila, who has a PhD in biodiversity. Pondering the difference between play and other animal behaviour, she notes: 'When playing, an animal usually tries to manipulate objects or … make new combinations of movements … not to directly [improve] its survival, but to learn about its own limits and abilities.'

I think about this in relation to my memory of setting up that little half-room as a writing office in my share house. I think of myself as an animal, manipulating objects – a three-piece pink velour lounge suite I found at a Salvation Army charity shop, along with an old wooden desk and a West German pottery vase to use as my pen jar – and making new combinations of movements to learn about my own limits and abilities. To learn – through the playful act of decorating an empty room to turn it into a writing space – that I could enjoy writing stories. That I wanted to do it because I love it and because it brings me joy.

Play is often seen as a worthless or unproductive way to spend our time. But cultivating a sense of playfulness is incredibly important for the profound effect it can have on our lives, and on others. So much of what we crave – connectedness, a sense of meaning and purpose, belonging – starts with play. It's through play that we learn and become curious. Curiosity feeds our ability to stay open – to ourselves and the world. Openness stimulates our powers of observation and ability to pay attention, to feel awe and wonder at the miraculous moments in every day of our lives. When we engage in play it not only brings us joy, but teaches us with profound power how we can learn and practise resilience, and meet our fears. Peter Gray, a psychologist focused on the role of play and curiosity in learning and education, says not indulging in play 'kills the spirit and stunts mental growth'.

Whether or not it's comfortable for us to acknowledge and engage in, play is a part of who we are as human beings. As a species. It's how we learn and thrive. Just like gulls, crocodiles, ravens, elephants, dogs …

Fear is in our wiring. And so is play.

In 2014, two of the books on creativity that I read when I was grieving the death of my family member were *Steal Like an Artist* and *Show Your Work*, both drawn and written by artist and writer Austin Kleon. I was moved by many points and phrases in both books, but one that cut through the fog and blur of grief and landed in an affecting way in my mind was his instruction in *Steal Like an Artist* to 'use your hands'. The chapter opens with the title in caps – STEP AWAY FROM THE SCREEN – and an observation that working on computers has 'robbed us of feeling that we're actually making things'.

Kleon goes on to make the case for the power of creating not just from and with our heads, but from and with our bodies. 'Bring your body into your work,' he exhorts us, pointing out that 'our bodies can tell our brains as much as our brains can tell our bodies'. He uses himself as an example, sharing how he reintroduced analogue tools into his process to make creating things 'fun again', and noticed his work start to improve as a result. Then he detailed how his office was set up, and reading this was the lightning strike for me: he wrote about having two desks in his office, an 'analogue' desk and a 'digital' desk. Anything electronic was banned from his analogue desk; it was purely for his drawing materials: pencils, markers, notebooks. On his digital desk were tech tools needed to edit and publish his work: laptop, tablet, monitor.

In the thick of grief and processing the shock of death and the totality of loss in our lives, reading about Kleon's office set-up sent pinwheels of colour shooting through my heart. I imagine that if we could have scanned my brain then, it would have been lit up like the Griswold house in December. At a time when I thought nothing would feel good again, I read about a stranger's two desks, one for making things with his hands and the other to do digital work, and it threw me the lifeline I didn't know I needed.

When I returned to my writing office, I got serious about getting playful with my office space and using my hands. I bought two secondhand desks online and used one purely for handwriting, and the other purely for typing. Arranging and stocking each desk brought me such deep and satisfying joy. Fountain pen, ink pot, oil burner, candles, matches, notebooks, talismans, flowers on analogue. Laptop, keyboard, printer, speakers on digital. Having both made even just going into my office feel like fun.

Not long after, it was at the analogue desk that I sat one day, maddened and emboldened by grief, and watched my hand write the opening sentence of *The Lost Flowers of Alice Hart*.

Holly's office, with analogue desk (left) and digital desk (right)

Engaging play has been one of the most powerful ways I've been able to find my way back to myself and to my inner country. When I'm writing and fear coils around my throat now, I often think about my kid self with her She-Ra sword, and choose play instead. That might mean that I decorate my writing space. Or I pick up crayons and draw (I am unskilled at drawing). Or I make a ritual of lighting candles and burning essential oils before I start to write. Sometimes I'll blare Pearl Jam and thrash about before writing. Sometimes I write in my pjs all day. Other times I've been known to show up at my desk in a red polka-dot dress with

74

Choose play instead.

my morning coffee in a martini glass. The point is: whatever it takes. The point is: play is how I've learned to give myself the joy of creating and free myself from living small.

Play is a powerful tool we are born with an instinct to use. How we play is universal, and individual. What play means and feels like for me might not be the same for you. But you have the instinct too.

If you don't know how to start or where to begin to remember or recover your sense of play, if self-doubt stops you, there is something you can practise right now that might help you find your way.

Self-compassion.

FEAR + PLAY PROVOCATIONS

1 How would creativity feel to you if there was no perceived risk, threat, failure, vulnerability or sense of shame around it?

2 What would you create if your sword was raised and no one was watching or judging you?

3 If there was no such thing as fear, what first action would you take towards answering the ideas knocking at the walls of your heart, asking to be made?

4 If you had the set-up of your dreams – a painting studio, a dance floor, a bakery kitchen, a library, an office, a garden – what's the first thing you would make?

G ① freeing
② Difficult
③ Trying / Experimenting
④ write a book

2

Self-doubt +
Self-compassion:
An Ancient Beauty

Two pivotal writing moments from my childhood. The first: I was three years old when Mum taught me to read and I told her I wanted to be an author. The second: I was ten years old, in primary school, Grade Six, 1990, and I lived for new *Baby-Sitters Club* books, and for collecting novelty-shaped erasers and fruit-scented, coloured-ink ballpoint pens. That was also the year when computing was introduced into our public-school curriculum, and touch-typing lessons on Toshiba laptops (roughly the size and weight of an old-fashioned telephone book) were integrated into our daily classes. Until then, all my stories had only ever been written by hand. There was something, a connection, between how I gripped my pencil while I wrote and the excitement and thrill that I felt while I was writing.

Learning to touch-type was one of the most exhilarating things that had ever happened in my first ten years of being alive. I took to it freakishly, speeding through multiple lessons in the time allotted for one. My fastest recorded speed was 111 words per minute. That year, 'motor skills and coordination' were applauded in my report card (the only time my coordination skills were ever academically praised). By learning to touch-type, I discovered something about myself that felt akin to uncovering a superpower: I found a way to keep up with my imagination. I could sit down at a computer and type the story in my mind in real time as it came to me. I never lost a sentence or forgot an idea because it was taking me too long to handwrite them. I learned to touch-type as fast as I could think.

In 1992, when I was eleven-turning-twelve, Mum bought me a refurbished IBM desktop computer and printer. We'd never had a computer game, let alone a personal computer in our home. 'So that you can write more stories,' Mum told me as we set up the IBM and printer in my bedroom. I hugged and thanked her profusely, but it didn't feel like enough – I didn't have the language to express what it meant to me. We were a working-class, single-parent family, and Mum worked herself thin to provide for us. Yet she found the means, financially and psychologically, to support my writing. For the next couple of years, writing fiction was how I survived changing family dynamics, the transition from primary school to high school, making new friends and trying to make sense of the wild potency of becoming a teenager.

The most sustained, free and joyful writing I've ever experienced was when I was fourteen, in 1994. Posters from *TV Hits* and *Rolling Stone* magazines on my bedroom wall: River Phoenix, Pearl Jam, East 17, The Cranberries, Boyz II Men, Salt-N-Pepa, Silverchair. I started writing my first novel, although I don't remember ever finishing it – not because I abandoned it but because it just wouldn't end. Tens of thousands of words long, it started out as a homage to River Phoenix (my first true love, may he rest in peace) heavily influenced by his film *Running On Empty* (micro-summary: the teenage son of an activist family on the run falls in love with the daughter of a wealthy, conservative family, and tormented love ensues). My novel then morphed into a fan-fiction mash-up of *Beverly Hills 90210* (Brenda and Dylan) and *Baywatch* (Eddie and Shauni), with threads from *Sweet Valley High* (Elizabeth Wakefield) and *Press Gang* (Spike and Lynda) thrown in for good measure. My god, I loved writing that story. Booting up my IBM and opening MS Word to escape into the world of it became my favourite way to spend my free time. My closest friends started reading and following the story like a serial. I printed them copies that we read together and discussed. I recall us all sitting in my bedroom, twitching and feverish with joy, as we gushed over a particular moment in my novel when the family mansion of our heroine blew up (of course) and she narrowly escaped with one of the catering staff, naturally a troubled loner, to start a beautiful, doomed new life with him on the run in Malibu (obviously). I couldn't write the next instalment fast enough – I just wrote whatever brought me the most joy to imagine and create.

During that time, while I was writing, I wasn't motivated by the idea of publishing the story. I don't recall that ever coming to mind. I also don't have any memory of judging my story as I wrote it. I wasn't plagued by self-doubt-fuelled thoughts like *Is this story shit? Is my writing shit? Am I shit? What if it's all shit?* I was a fourteen-year-old girl, and one true thing that I knew about myself was that I loved making up and writing stories, for no reason other than the pleasure it brought me. My inner country was vast, thriving, wild, full of life, and being in it, dreaming and creating and writing from that place, made me happier than most other things. I wrote, never wondering if I was silly or naïve for trying to write. That novel was the best thing I'd ever written at that point in my life, because I absolutely loved the bejesus out of it. There was no question in my mind about whether it was worth my time.

Of course, being fourteen, I wasn't financially independent. I didn't have adult responsibilities. My brain hadn't matured enough to understand how important the escapism I found in my writing then was for me and my development. But the experience of creating for pure joy, of writing just because I loved it, left such a deep mark on me that it would haunt me for years afterwards when I was so full of self-doubt that I couldn't write a word.

My late teens were hard, as they are for so many of us. It didn't take much to chip away at my self-confidence and self-esteem: years of difficult change in my family, transitional friendships and then a brutal teenage relationship breakup left me with very little self-worth. After I finished high school, I submitted my writing to competitions and for publication in various anthologies and journals but didn't place or get accepted. In my eyes, I'd tried and failed at my dream of becoming a writer, which, on top of the rejection and shame I was already carrying, was too painful to acknowledge. Not equipped with the mental tools or strategies to understand or process self-doubt and self-worth, I pushed those emotions away. My creativity was a lost world to me. As Sylvia Plath wrote, 'The worst enemy to creativity is self-doubt.' Depleted, I numbed myself to feeling grief and didn't realise that by doing so I also became numb to feeling authentic, meaningful joy.

By the time I turned twenty-one, the act of writing, the source of my truest sense of identity, connection, joy and meaning, had become an abandoned ghost-self, stuffed away into neglected corners of my mind.

It would be another eight years before I wrote freely again, when I sat at my desk after my session with Mary, writing a short story through the night, then felt a flood of joyous recognition return to me as golden dawn light washed over my keyboard.

Broadly, self-doubt can be described as a state of mind that can result from negative experiences in the past, in relationships, situations or circumstances, when who we are or how we behave has been criticised or shamed by others. If we've been told we fall short or are incompetent, our self-worth can suffer severely, sooner or later in life. We can also find that the pressures of society for us to succeed can do us more harm than good.

To protect ourselves from the pain of feeling shame or failure, we learn to doubt ourselves, to doubt our capacity and ability to experience anything new or unfamiliar in any valuable kind of way. When it comes to creativity, self-doubt can manifest in a myriad of intrusive thoughts:

I doubt taking a painting class would be worth your time and money. What if you make a fool of yourself? You've never even picked up a paint brush.

You won't manage hosting and cooking that dinner party for your friend's birthday. Remember the last time you tried? You ended up ordering takeaway.

You might start a novel but you'll never finish it. You're not that talented. You don't have the commitment and guts to see it through.

You can't pull off wearing a raspberry-coloured suit to that event. It's too much. You're too much. Everyone is just going to look at you.

I doubt you should join the community garden group. You don't know anyone and it's so hard to make friends. The other gardeners are probably experts, unlike you.

When the sign-up form for singing classes says 'all beginners welcome', they don't mean your level of beginner. You're whatever comes before a beginner.

If we're in the chokehold of self-doubting thoughts like these, is it any wonder that when we approach the unknown landscape of our untapped creativity, we're blasted with the same core message: YOU WON'T BE ABLE TO DO IT, SO DON'T EVEN TRY.

To doubt ourselves is to be human. Some degree of self-doubt is healthy. It's important to question ourselves, to stay open and be curious about our thinking. To learn about how we react and respond to unfamiliar situations and circumstances, and to be honest with ourselves about our behaviour. It's important to continue learning about who we are when we're comfortable, and uncomfortable. Self-doubt also keeps us safe from making decisions that are mortally threatening, such as bungee jumping off a bridge for the first time without expert guidance.

But, unmanaged, self-doubt can become a rampant, toxic force in our lives. When we listen to thoughts fuelled by self-doubt and believe them to be true, when we make choices based on those mistruths about ourselves, our full potential to feel, create and experience joy and connection is stolen from us. Our curiosity and sense of adventure about ourselves and what we're capable of are diminished. And so often we wrongly believe we're powerless to stop doubting ourselves.

In the past, when I've wanted to write but unchecked self-doubt has stopped me, the consequences of my actions going undone – aside from having nothing written on paper – have often been physical. That kind of overpowering self-doubt is a cold and numb sensation in my body. Hair-raising, as if there's something over my shoulder that I won't look at. A brittle, hypervigilant state. My heart races and I can't think clearly. I can't settle. There's an anvil at my temple. A crawling sensation in my skin. When I'm overpowered by self-doubt, it feels like fear with the cold-shock quality of broken trust. Because I feel abandoned. But not just by anyone. By myself. I've broken my own trust. That's the deep damage that self-doubt can wreak upon on us if we don't learn to manage it: we abandon the truest and purest parts of ourselves.

But, as the saying often attributed to Anaïs Nin goes, the time comes when the risk of remaining tight in a bud is more painful than the risk it takes to blossom. Self-doubt and my negligible sense of self-worth kept me tightly bound and small for most of my twenties, no matter how much I thought the way to 'fix' myself was to focus on just 'being happy'. That bind only started to loosen in my thirties, when I began to learn that self-doubt wasn't something to get rid of but a part of myself I could learn to embrace. I started to wonder: if self-doubt felt like abandonment, what would the opposite feel like? An instant scene played out in my mind, one we've seen in the movies or known first-hand, of being in a crowded room, vulnerable, unsure of ourselves, alone and awkward with a sinking feeling in our hearts, when we suddenly lock eyes with someone. They offer a friendly smile. And say something like, 'You can sit here.'

Sweet relief: that's what the opposite of abandoning myself felt like. Accompanying and befriending myself. Being my own refuge. I wanted to stop warring with myself and just be on my own fucking side. It felt like there was a canyon, though, between where I was, full of self-doubt, and where I wanted to be – able to manage self-doubt and write. Able to feel like I could take agency of my mind and free myself from fear-based decision-making. I was sick of the overpowering thought in my mind being *I can't do it.*

It took the death of my family member to finally put my fear and self-doubt into perspective. Grief and loss can do many merciless things to our lives. But, by contrast, they can also show us that things we thought we'd lost inside ourselves have been there waiting for us to find them all along. As I've mentioned, in grief I reached out for books about creativity and writing. Austin Kleon's, and also Julia Cameron's iconic and widely beloved *The Artist's Way*, a twelve-week program designed to help artists unblock themselves and create. When I embarked on the program in the weeks and months after my family member died, the canyon between abandoning myself and accompanying myself started to close.

I read widely around creativity, trauma, self-doubt, self-esteem, self-confidence and self-worth. By following *The Artist's Way*, I remembered the kid in me who loved writing stories. As in, I *really* remembered that kid. My young hands, the bluebird signet ring I wore until it broke. The view of the sky from my writing desk in my childhood bedroom. The intoxicating smell of timber, crayons and pencil shavings every time I opened my desk lid. The feeling of a clean, fresh blank page in an exercise book. The innocence, naïveté, hope, love and grief in my heart. The places where I found stories: down by the sea, in the pastel colours of a perfectly whole scallop shell, or in my mum's garden, between the fronds of ferns.

I remembered that kid and reached across the canyon for her. I took the risk. And so started the process of unfurling that tight bud.

In 2014 when I was thirty-four years old and sat in wild exasperation, grief and determination at my writing desk, I asked myself:

What would happen if for just ten minutes you tried to write, and for once didn't listen to all the reasons you can't do it?

What if for once you came from that place inside, where you used to make up stories as naturally as you took breath? What would your kid self do if she was sitting at this desk?

I took the lid off my pen. I was shaking.

As I watched my hand write the opening line of *The Lost Flowers of Alice Hart* in my notebook, I wasn't fully aware that I'd just chosen an act of self-compassion over self-doubt, but by doing so, in that moment, by some immeasurable degree, my relationship with myself changed.

Kristin Neff is a pioneer in the study of self-compassion. She writes that, at its heart, self-compassion is giving ourselves the same care and kindness we'd give to a close friend. She further explains: 'Self-compassion is one of the most powerful sources of coping and resilience we have available to us.'

Learning how to treat myself and my creativity as I would treat a good friend and their creativity was astonishingly effective, and incredibly hard. I was so used to abandoning myself when I felt like I'd made a mistake, or something I'd pursued hadn't worked out, or I'd not met someone's expectations, or I'd perceived myself to have failed at something I tried. Those were all examples and evidence upon which years of self-doubt had been built. To reconstruct them took effort, will and vulnerability, which I tried desperately to avoid feeling. But it's an unyielding question: are you treating yourself the way you'd treat your best friend and their creativity?

In 2016, while I was rewriting the draft of *The Lost Flowers of Alice Hart*, I was struggling with fear, post-traumatic stress and anxiety. Unable to stand the noise of self-doubt blasting through my mind, I wrote down my thoughts to get them out of my head. Reading them in cold light on paper, I was shocked by their viciousness. Practising self-compassion, I tried imagining myself saying the same things to Libby, my best friend for more than two decades. Imagining myself speaking to Libby in the same way I did to myself about her creativity – her watercolour paintings, pot-plant arrangements, essential oil blends, cooking – was truly horrifying. From then on, whenever I started to notice cruel judgements creeping into my mind, I dismantled their power by giving them what I called 'The Libby Test'. Would I speak to Libby that way about her creativity? Every single time, the answer was, *Fuck no.*

Over time I noticed that I intuitively moved on to imagining saying such things to my kid self as she sat at her desk, daydreaming and writing her stories. Can you imagine? I played with the concept further, extending the exercise to include my beloved, precious niece and nephews. I imagined them immersed in their joy when drawing, collaging, painting, dancing, writing stories, making Lego shapes. Imagined myself responding to their creativity in the same way I did to my own. Try imagining it with a small person you know. It's absurd. To think about saying to any child, *Who do you think you are, trying to make this? Why would you even try when it's not going to get you anywhere in life? You're only going to find out you can't do it in the end, so why even bother trying? This 'art' you've made is total shit. You might as well just give up. What a waste of time.* I couldn't and can't bear the thought.

Playing out that scenario caused me to wonder why I accepted my own fierce questioning of my creativity.

Beginning to practise self-compassion, to go inward with self-acceptance and a refusal to abandon myself through discomfort, caused a reckoning. I had to confront and acknowledge that before I'd learned that there was another way − before I'd understood that I could treat myself with kindness rather than judgement − I'd allowed self-doubt to minimise my life and creativity. I was haunted by the thought of the countless times I'd told myself, *You can't do this*, and I'd listened. This was a hard realisation to come to terms with, that there'd always been another way. Instead of self-doubt, I could have met myself with encouragement, support and self-compassion.

Rather than feel bitter about this, rather than feed self-doubt even more, the practice of self-compassion means that I soften towards all of those missed years of my stories that went unwritten, and the ways that writing them could have enriched my life. I soften towards that past version of me. I was doing my best at the time. I didn't know what I didn't know. I wasn't fully aware of how low my self-worth was, or how hard self-doubt was working to stop me from trying so that I wouldn't be at risk. In that way, self-compassion has given me an ability to understand that even in all its reductive power, self-doubt stems from an instinct to self-protect.

I've been consciously practising self-compassion for six years now. To me, it's about staying with yourself instead of abandoning yourself in discomfort. So I soften. Towards accepting the humanness of doubting myself and the power of staying with myself in wild discomfort. When self-doubt rises, I follow the advice of Myf Jones, author and beloved friend: I pat self-doubt on the head. As if it is a loyal scrounging little creature that we can always expect to show up, uninvited. Pat, pat, pat. I hold my gaze unwaveringly on knowing that the choice not to abandon myself is mine. I choose to give myself compassion in any given moment. I choose to never again let self-doubt be the driving force in my creativity.

One of my favourite movies when I was ten and learning to touch-type was the American film *Big*, starring Tom Hanks. It's about Josh Baskin, a pre-teen boy who goes to a carnival with his friends and, after being denied access to a ride because he's too short, finds a fortune-telling machine called Zoltar. Josh inserts his quarter and makes his wish to be big. After receiving a card saying his wish has been granted, Josh discovers Zoltar was unplugged the whole time. The next morning when Josh wakes up, he's no longer a pre-teen but an adult. The entire film delighted me, but, at ten years old, the moment that wholly captured my imagination was Josh's interaction with Zoltar.

An element of making art that constantly awes me is that so often it's only through our creative expression – in my case, writing – that we can make any truthful sense of ourselves. It's not until right now, as I write this, that I'm realising a game I've played in my mind with myself for about fifteen years stems from how awestruck I was as a kid watching Zoltar in all its mystery and possibility. The game is one I call Bullshit-o-Meter. Not quite as alluring as Zoltar, but it works for me. I play Bullshit-o-Meter when I need to check in with my deeper self about how I'm really doing. My check-in might be about writing, or vulnerability, or fear, or rest. Sometimes when I use Bullshit-o-Meter to have a deep check-in with myself, the outcome is super tender and full of self-kindness. Sometimes I realise I'm teetering on burnout and

What if self-doubt stems from an instinct to self-protect?

need to prioritise rest. Or that my mind is overloaded and fragile and I need to go gently until I feel stronger. But when I use Bullshit-o-Meter to check in with myself and it catches a whiff of a lie? It becomes the greatest pastiche of sports coaches with big hearts and bad language ever known:

BULLSHIT-O-METER: Roll up, roll up, place your palm here, and have your truth told!

ME: *[Places palm where instructed]*

BULLSHIT-O-METER: Speak your deep truth!

ME: *[Sighs.]* I just can't write today, I'm soooo busy, I don't have time to get anything substantial down, so, yeah, I'm just not going to bother with even the ten minutes I have spare to jot down ideas. There's no point. They'll be shit anyway. Tomorrow's a new day. I'll think about writing then.

BULLSHIT-O-METER: *[Lights up as palm is scanned]* Your thoughts have been read for a deep-truth check-in!

ME: *[Holds breath]*

BULLSHIT-O-METER: Your thoughts are … bullshit, Ringles! And, deep down, you know that. So let's stop fucking about, shall we? Remember your fucking joy, remember what you're fucking made of, and make your time today fucking count. As you well know, even ten minutes spent with your notebook can bring an idea to life. Yay! Your imagination needs you to do its magic. Go forth! Thanks for using Bullshit-o-Meter for another deep-truth check-in.

Holly discovering a fortune-telling Zoltar Speaks machine in Southport, UK

ME: *[Huffs and skulks off to get notebook, loving and hating the power of Bullshit-o-Meter.]*

Outcome: I write for those ten minutes and, more often than not, connect new dots I've never noticed before about an idea that's been kicking around in my mind for a while.

There are, of course, myriad things we can't choose. Inequalities are not an individual choice. A panic attack is not a choice. Patterns of post-traumatic stress are not a choice. Grief is not a choice. Anxiety is not a choice.

But managing to treat ourselves with compassion can be a choice. Available to us at any moment of any day. Over and over and over again.

Something I think about often: every single piece of art ever made at any time in human existence that you've ever loved so much you think it's going to make your heart combust – every song, movie, moment in a video game, painting, photograph, page of writing, piece of music, mouthful of food, dance choreography, lyric, speech, performance – has gone through some kind of wash with the creator's self-doubt.

And yet. It exists.

I am reminded of the words of Van Gogh: 'If you hear a voice within you say, "You cannot paint," then by all means paint, and that voice will be silenced.'

It's all about creating despite the doubt. Just … creating.

While I was writing *The Lost Flowers of Alice Hart* in Manchester, I'd spend hours researching Australian native flowers for the story, particularly ones I remembered from my time living in the desert. When my memories of those flowers in the red dirt became too much for me, I'd step away from my desk and take my thoughts outside, to a nearby park that I loved, full of cherry blossom trees.

On one such walk, brimming with an electric sense of wonder at the explosions of dense candy-pink blossoms in bloom, I climbed into the boughs of a cherry blossom tree and lay there a while. Looking up and around at the riot of blossoms, I thought about the tree's ancient beauty, so beautifully described by Toi Derricotte in her poem 'Cherry Blossoms', and how different – bare and lifeless – it looked in winter from its raucous and joyous abundance in spring. Lying in the boughs, my mind swirled with images of malukuru/desert peas, ininti/bat's wing coral trees, kaliny-kalinypa/honey grevillea, kurkara/desert oaks, and the conditions they needed to seed and bloom. I thought about how flowers and trees don't experience self-doubt. In the right conditions, they bloom, or, if the conditions aren't right, they don't. What a cherry blossom tree doesn't ever do is question whether it's a shit tree, or if it has shit flowers. It blooms. Because that's what a cherry tree does.

A cherry blossom tree doesn't stop itself from blooming each spring in case its flowers might not be good enough.

A cherry blossom tree isn't stunted by a fear of failure.

It has its seasons. As do we.

Nothing is wasted in its life cycles. Nor in ours.

Creativity is how we can bloom.

Holly in her favourite cherry blossom tree, Manchester, UK

SELF-DOUBT + SELF-COMPASSION PROVOCATIONS

1. What would you create if you didn't listen to your self-doubt for five minutes, ten minutes, one hour, one day, one week?

2. What would it feel like to follow your creative joy and surround it with the support, encouragement and kindness a best friend would show you?

3. How might your creativity be affected if self-compassion rather than self-doubt directed your mindset?

If you had a creativity check-in with Bullshit-o-Meter, or your own version of Zoltar, and told it all the reasons you might have for not creating, for not blooming, what would your Bullshit-o-Meter's compassionate response be?

1. You don't feel to treate anything

2. No idea

3. Positively

3

Failure + Nothing is Wasted: A Door to the Wild

After I left the desert, the overwhelming sense I had of my life was one of irrefutable defeat. I'd had to uproot myself from the landscape, and the life I'd made there. I grappled with how deeply I felt I'd failed by leaving.

I never threw a goodbye party to honour the place and people who'd made living on the red dirt among the kurkara/desert oaks so meaningful to me. I didn't give a proper handover to the person who took on my job. I didn't get to thank or farewell those who were most important to me, or explain why I was leaving, and I didn't get to visit beloved places one last time, to score them in my memory, that way we do when we're closing a chapter in our lives. None of these things might have mattered to anyone else — transience was familiar in the desert community — but these things mattered to me. And I'd failed in all of them.

Back in my childhood hometown, failure and shame were a combined invasive force that I felt consume my body. It pounded behind my eyes. My shoulders seemed to curl inwards from the pressure of it. Every step shook with the strain of carrying it. I struggled often with short-term memory loss and the sense that I wasn't in my body but was somehow bobbing along beside myself, like a floating helium balloon. Jane, the psychologist I first met with after I left the desert, helped me to learn and understand that I was experiencing dissociation, the mind's way of cutting off and protecting itself from things too hard to process, often resulting in symptoms including an out-of-body feeling and memory issues.

During one session, Jane asked me if I was making any new friends after life in the desert. My mum has always told me I don't have a poker face; I didn't need to speak to give Jane her answer. 'Making new friends can be scary,' she said, 'but having the courage to invest in just one new connection with a person will be of immeasurable benefit to your life.'

A few months later I moved interstate to a new city for a new job, where I started seeing my next psychologist, Mary. But I remembered Jane's words. *Just one new connection.*

I got lucky. I didn't find just one new friend who changed my life. I found three.

When I first moved to the new city, I needed a place to stay while I got settled. After my new work colleagues asked around, Elfie, as we're going to call her, responded, saying that I, a stranger, could move into the spare room of her flat. All we knew about each other was that we were roughly the same age (mid to late twenties), both working for the same organisation, and, according to testimonies from mutual acquaintances, neither of us were axe murderers.

Meeting Elfie was, without exaggeration, love at first sight: we laughed, cried, hugged, hung out on the couch, drank tea, ate a meal and spoke things aloud to each other that we couldn't divulge to anyone else. Elfie had also moved to the new city for a new start. She had her story, and I had mine. Over the coming weeks, we took road trips, went swimming in the sea, and, when the outside world was too much, curled up in quiet heaviness together. Living with Elfie for that short time before I found my own place brought me home to myself somehow. She was the first person I'd told in a long time about the knowledge I'd carried within me since I was three years old: *I want to be a writer.* My friendship with Elfie began to clear some of the dense, trauma-induced fog in my mind. Thanks to her love, attention and care, I began to remember parts of myself

I'd forgotten. That I was funny sometimes. That I had imaginative ideas. That I was a good friend. I began to remember who I was beneath the ashes of everything I'd left behind in the desert. The weight of shame and failure pressing on my heart shifted slightly. Elfie gave me the confidence to look other people in the eye when they smiled at me at work or made polite chit chat. Or, as was the case when I met Nick, let myself genuinely belly laugh.

Nick and I worked in the same department in our jobs. I've just texted him to confirm that our very first contact with each other was during a board meeting, which was as bland and dry as it sounds. I instinctively made myself small to fit in. But there was something about Nick that immediately made my senses perk up and pay attention. Unlike everyone else gathered around the table, whenever we made brief eye contact, I caught something in Nick's expression. It was a twitch to his smile, a twinkle in his eyes. A spark. By which I really mean a glorious neon wildfire of spirit. After the board meeting, when I was asked to go to his desk to collect some papers, I felt an immediate incandescent joy tear through me. The kind of feeling you get when you're drawn to a person by instinct and connection, by some kind of recognition that they're your kind of someone. As Nick was mine, and I was his.

Through Nick, I met Matty, whose laughter was like a defibrillator to my being the first time I heard it. I drew near to them both like they were a blazing fire on a frozen night. Over the next nine or so months, these two men loved me back into being. By demanding I leave my bedroom, despite my protestations, for nights that ended up with me dressed as Britney Spears on a dance floor. By joining me at after-work yoga classes – the three of us were the juvenile idiots giggling up the back while doing downward dog poses. They took me out on fancy dinner dates to swanky restaurants, or, when all of us needed sanctuary, we plonked in a pillow fort on one of their couches for *Melrose Place* marathons. They invited me to be their date to Bushdance, one of the biggest annual events on the local community calendar; I twirled around the dance floor in my cowboy boots, nearly peeing my pants with joy as I learned to 'strip the willow'.

Nick and Matty introduced me to their families and closest friends. They walked me into a sex shop for the first time in my life because, as they told me, I was 'twenty-nine, hot and single, not dead'. They cared for me, included me in their lives and loved me back into being by gently and firmly, with no-nonsense expressions on their faces, telling me hard home truths that I needed to hear about self-respect.

Allowing myself to be loved by Nick and Matty, and loving them with the full force of my heart, saturated my life with new colour, vivacity and joy. I started to feel like there was more to me than everything trauma, failure and shame had leached from my sense of self-value. Nick and Matty's friendship returned joy to me as a safe thing to feel in my body. The power of being around them, the power of feeling the joy of our togetherness, had a life-changing, flow-on effect. Because of their belief in me, I dared to remember how to believe in myself: I wanted to write without shame or failure stopping me. Because of their encouragement, I dared to research creative writing courses that would take me half the world away from my life in Australia. And from them.

Nevertheless, they championed me. Nick and Matty were the first to read the writing portfolio I slowly and shakily put together for my application to study for the MA in Creative Writing at Manchester.

When I thought there was nothing in my life or myself to offer to anyone or anything, the love of three new people I met at a pivotal time, along with the support of my closest family and friends, reminded me that while shame and failure are very real and powerful forces, they didn't have to be total or definitive.

Left to right: Nick, Holly and Matty, Bushdance

Even while we are ashamed and feel like failures, even when we think we have nothing to offer, we can still choose. Choose to make something new from nothing.

In an article for *Harvard Business Review*, Peter Sims, author of *Little Bets: How Breakthrough Ideas Emerge from Small Discoveries*, argues that creativity and innovation require us to stop obsessing about 'failure' and to start thinking instead about 'learning'. He goes on to give examples of how entrepreneurs and designers do just this – reject failure – and instead embrace making a lot of mistakes and 'little bets' to learn what works for them. The most powerful and impactful question the article asks is, 'How do you personally define a "failure"?'

Sims writes that if we've maybe gone bankrupt in a company we started, or we've been fired for values-breaking conduct, or we've left someone at the altar because we didn't listen to and honour the truth in our hearts, then yes, we have experienced a failure, and with that he can empathise. His next point is a knockout: 'However, if your internalised view of failure is anything that is not perfect, then you are disempowering yourself from exercising your inherent creativity.'

To answer Peter Sims's question – 'How do you personally define a "failure"?' – I've thought back over what I have written throughout my life. Whenever I've felt like my writing has failed,

Make something new from nothing.

what I realise I've been feeling is shame that it wasn't 'perfect'. Perfectionism is a sneaky, shape-shifting member of the Fear family and can show up masked as failure.

In my earlier years as a writer, my sense of being a failure was (surprise!) often the most overwhelming when I was up to my neck in a first draft. Some utterly irrational and not entirely conscious part of my mind expected that I would sit down and write a perfect story, first go. I knew it was a ridiculous and unfair expectation to have of myself: when I put it through the Libby Test, it's not something I would ever expect of her, or anyone else's, creative process. Yet I still expected it of myself, and my creativity suffered, not thrived, because of it. Hello, internalised perfectionism.

This is one of the most important things I can tell you: creativity is a process. This shouldn't be something we have to learn, or be reminded of, but somehow it is. I have to remind myself every single time I sit down to write. Creativity is a process. A cake isn't baked in one step. A sculpture isn't created with one touch on clay. A novel isn't written in one day. Creating anything is a process, and writing first drafts is no exception. Maybe the single most powerful thing I've learned about being a writer is that a first draft, in all its absolute mess and shitfulness, is actually perfect – all it needs to do is exist. All I need a first draft to do is hold the seeds of the story that I've put down on paper, while I go away to think about it, come back, go away, come back, over and over and over again through a process of revision, to nurture and grow those seeds until they split open, reach for the sun and bloom.

An aside: it's important to acknowledge that I'm writing this book as a working artist. Since 2018, my writing has become my livelihood. Nevertheless, this book isn't about how to make money from our creativity, nor does it define failure as an inability to earn cold hard cash to pay our rent and feed and clothe ourselves.

This book is about giving ourselves whatever permission, time and space we need to create, simply because making stuff is good for us. Creativity enriches our sense of meaning and agency in our lives; strengthens our confidence and empowerment; cultivates resilience; fosters compassion for and connection with others; stimulates empathy; allows us to express ourselves in ways we otherwise can't; encourages us to stay curious, open-minded and open-hearted; and boosts our mental health and wellbeing. This book is about creating because, for all the reasons just mentioned, creativity allows us to access and give ourselves joy. Not just dopamine-laced, endorphin-rich joy, but the kind of joy that Ross Gay and Audre Lorde and Toi Derricotte write about – respectively, joy as the connecting of our sorrows, shared joy that lessens the threat of our differences, and joy as an act of resistance.

Writing this book as someone whose creativity has become their paycheque is an incredibly privileged and lucky position to be in. Yet, I wouldn't have had anything to submit to publishers in 2016 if I hadn't spent the preceding two, three, four, ten years of my life trying to find the guts to give myself permission to write just because I loved it. And to write from that place of love, not fear, as my source. That place of joy and hope, that tender, beautiful, lush place inside all of us. Writing from there, from my inner country, is what has changed the way I live.

To think more generally about how we define failure in our creativity, we need to go back to basics and be clear about why we create.

If we stop fearing failure, and focus instead on learning, as Peter Sims suggests, then it becomes simpler. We want to be creative because it simply brings us joy to make stuff. To make something out of nothing. It makes us happy to be in our imagination, to explore and follow our instincts without overthinking them, and to develop our skills in our creative practice. So if our aim is to engage with creativity because it brings us joy, how the fuck can we actually fail at it?

But I know very well first-hand that this is exactly how we can feel. We're robbed of the joy of creating by the fear of whatever we create not emerging perfectly, and by the feeling that if it's not perfect, by whatever standard, then we're failures. I wouldn't expect this perfectionism from anyone else's creative process. Again, I ask myself, why do I accept it for my own?

In 2019, Libby started taking pottery classes. She'd never worked with clay before. I watched in awe and joy as she shared with me her process of learning and practising to shape her clay, firing the kiln, and mixing and applying glaze. I didn't once look at Libby's pottery creations and think to myself, let alone say to her, *Geez, it's not coming out perfect, Libs. Sorry, you're obviously a total failure at pottery.* It was the opposite: I deeply loved her creations in all their tactile, characteristic, imperfect beauty.

A question: if we went into our kitchen / showed up at our writing desk / went into our garden / stood in front of a blank canvas / opened a visual diary to a blank page / poured mosaic glass on a benchtop, aiming to make time for our creativity and to give ourselves joy through the act of honouring the weird, glorious beauty of having an imagination, then, just by showing up, haven't we achieved that aim?

Some more questions:

No matter what it is that we've made – a burnt cake, a short story full of inconsistencies, a knitted scarf riddled with dropped stitches, an out-of-time choreography – isn't it precisely because of our 'imperfect' creation that we've *learned* more about ourselves and our creative process? That we've learned something – about ourselves, our art, our practice – that we wouldn't have if we'd not made anything at all?

Can we fail if the act of honouring our creativity and giving ourselves joy is our aim?

Final follow-up question: Is it more accurate to say that the only way we fail at creativity is by not creating anything at all?

When it comes to creativity (and life in general) I suspect I'm not the only one who struggles to stop worrying about failure and instead focus on learning. Avoiding any scenario that shows our imperfections is more common that most of us think. So many of us were pressed by our parents and teachers to achieve and succeed, in school, in sports and in other pursuits such as playing musical instruments. And it continues in our working lives. It's always about getting the answers right, achieving perfection; seldom are you allowed to fail, experiment, innovate.

Feeling like a failure physically hurts. It aches in my shoulders and back. It curdles in my stomach and feels like embarrassment, disappointment, humiliation, hopelessness and worthlessness. It makes my eyes heavy and my face hot. It feels like foolishness for wanting something, for trying for something and not meeting expectations. Failure prickles my skin, leaves me cold and ties my mind in knots. It feels like shame. Like confirmation of the fear that I'm not enough. Most often, failure feels like a waste.

For the past decade, when I've been afraid of failing, one thing that has brought me untold comfort in my writing practice has been to remind myself that in the natural world failure doesn't exist. Everything becomes something else. Or, as inventor and professor Veena Sahajwalla says, 'In nature there is no such thing as garbage, it's a series of complex circular ecosystems where everything has a purpose, and nothing is left to waste – so why should our lives be any different?'

Dear reader, this is where I present to you the humble dung beetle. Dung beetles are part of the scarab family and are well known for the fact that they specifically feed on faeces. That's right. These little beetles depend upon another animal's waste for their survival. They can't exist without literal shit.

I love the different categories that dung beetles fall into, each one of which uses shit in its own way. Many dung beetles are known as rollers. Rollers roll dung into spherical balls that are then used as a source of food, or for breeding chambers. Other dung beetles called tunnellers bury the dung wherever they find it; some species can bury an amount of dung 250 times their own weight in just one night. A third group of dung beetles, known as dwellers, don't roll or bury dung at all. They just live in it. Dwellers simply need shit to live in.

So think of the dung beetle the next time you sit frustrated at your desk or workbench or in your studio. When something you've tried has not worked out and you're left with – you think – a pile of words, material, paint, wood or ingredients that are not coming together. And you're cursing them for being shit and berating yourself for your 'failure'.

But of course it's not a failure. The shit is useful. The shit is necessary. The shit can be rolled up and made into something else. This is the work of creativity. Nothing is wasted. We've learned and we'll keep learning.

As if the aforementioned species of dung beetle didn't offer our creativity enough metaphoric value in terms of demonstrating how nothing is wasted and everything can be reused, we then come to the nocturnal African dung beetle. It is reportedly one of the few invertebrates that navigates and orients itself by the light of the Milky Way. Even when we're surrounded by shit, it pays to keep our eyes on the stars. Even when we're buried deep in shit, there are miracles and magic to be found.

Living half a house away from mine in Manchester, England, is my dear friend, Laura. I call her an alchemist; she calls herself a metalsmith. Laura handmakes jewellery from ethically sourced recycled metals and gemstones. Being in her studio is like being in some kind of wonderland: drawers of gemstones in every colour, and tools, machines, cloths, ointments, patinas and polishes scattered across her workbench, all waiting to be used to create intricate, meaningful adornments.

One morning in 2019, I was sitting in Laura's workshop trying on some of her most recently made treasures while she was working on a bezel for a new pendant.

'Fuck it,' she sighed. I asked her what was wrong. She explained that the edges on the bezel had melted. I felt empathetically crushed for her. All her morning's work and concentration had been melted by her own hand, in front of her own eyes. I asked if she was okay.

'It happens,' she said with a shrug. 'All the time. Something might melt like this, which I can't know until it happens, or bits of a design won't align, or I might accidentally damage a shank or something like that, and it's really fucking annoying, especially if I'm in a groove. But it's just part of the making process.'

I asked if the melted bezel was fixable. She inspected it closely and shook her head. 'Into the scrap pot it goes.'

My ears pricked up. What was the scrap pot?

Laura's face lit up with her smile. 'It's my pot of fuck-ups and offcuts. Every now and then I fossick through it, pick up an odd-shaped piece, a mistake, and wonder what else it might want to be. So I melt it down, then end up turning it into stars or moons or flowers or any other embellishment I use in my designs.'

She showed me then how she uses her jewellery torch to melt down a tarnished bit of old silver. I watched, transfixed, as under the blue flame the silver liquified, glowed, changed shape and later cooled, waiting for Laura to make it into something new.

The day I left the desert by plane, I had a window seat on my departing flight. My shoulders shook as I watched the world that had been my life there shrink to minutiae after takeoff: the roof of my house, the plants in my garden, my favourite kurkara/

desert oaks, all abandoned, fading from my view in the sky. I believed I would never be able to return. I believed the only way to survive the grief, trauma and sense of shame and failure was to turn my back on that life and try never to think about it again. *Keep moving forward*, I used to tell myself. *Don't look back at what was wasted.*

Many years later, I don't think that way anymore. It's a startling reminder that as humans we are never fixed, always learning and able in any given moment to change our minds.

The years I spent living in the desert were some of the most enriching, challenging and transformative times of my life. I thought leaving there would break me. It didn't.

There was more love waiting for me than I could have fathomed. Like Laura's jewellery, I was melted down but I remade myself. Stronger.

I just took a break from writing to make a cuppa. I closed my eyes while the kettle boiled and called my favourite kurkara/desert oaks back to mind, two particular trees I would seek out most days after work, when I would wander the desert landscape at dusk. They were tall, old and regal, with long sweeping branches and soft needles. I would often stop to stand between the two of them and listen to the desert breeze, to the sounds as the sun set and sent colours streaking across the unencumbered sky. I would stand

and look up at their strong branches. They were grandmotherly in character, and just as enchanting.

As I made my cuppa, I remembered: those kurkara/desert oaks, in all their splendour, first began in fire. As seeds split open by flames.

Everything that I thought was wasted; everything and everyone I thought I'd failed; every goodbye I never had; every ounce of love and gratitude I never got to express – all of it came with me that day in 2014 when I sat down at my writing desk and reached across the canyon to the kid in me, full of dreams and unwritten stories. All of it came with me when I wrote the first line of *The Lost Flowers of Alice Hart*. When I kept showing up at my desk to write Alice's story, day after day after day. Slowly, I learned, with every word, with every bit of hope and grief and love and trauma that I poured onto the page: nothing is wasted.

In 2018, I was walking down the street in Clifden, Ireland. I was staying nearby in Connemara on a research trip for my second novel. I had driven my rental car into Clifden for a necessary pint of Guinness at the pub, a browse of the local bookshop and a peek in the family-owned jewellery store on the street corner, with display windows full of symbols from Celtic mythology and folklore cast in gold, silver and gemstones. As I approached the jewellery store, I saw it: a curious tiny door set into the wall on the side of the shop, a few centimetres above the footpath. The door had a windowpane and little curtains, even a tiny line of faux grass at the threshold. Inside the jewellery store, I asked the owners about it.

'It's our fairy door,' they answered, deadpan.

'Fairy door,' I repeated. 'Got yourselves direct access to Fairyland?' I waited for them to indulge my playfulness. They didn't.

'It's a door between this world and the Otherworld,' they answered. 'It's important to give the fairies access to come and go, and to remind ourselves that the Otherworld exists. Everyone suffers otherwise.'

Baffled, I could only smile. I bought a silver pendant of flying swans and drove home, lost in my thoughts. Away with the fairies, if you will. Long into that night, I read about doors between worlds in Irish culture, gripped with fascination by the thought of them not just benefiting the fairies, giving them access to come and go between worlds, but being a reminder of another realm that exists beyond our own.

That same night I read the W.B. Yeats poem 'The Stolen Child', about a fairy stealing a child away to the fairy world to give it respite from the senseless suffering of the human world:

For he comes, the human child,
To the waters and the wild
With a faery, hand in hand,
For the world's more full of weeping than he can understand.

I was struck by the conviction in the poem that there was another world we could escape to, where it was possible to seek solace and build resilience. And I thought again about imagination. The world of it. The place we can go to in our minds, inside ourselves, where, as Carl Jung said, the hours pass like minutes. That other world. That wild, inner land.

'If you have a deep scar,' psychoanalyst Clarissa Pinkola Estés wrote, 'that is a door. If you yearn for a … full life … that is a door.' What if our scars and yearnings are doorways that open inwards, to that wild place? *Second to the right, and straight on till morning.*

What if failures are our directions to the place inside where we can find sanctuary in our imagination and in our hopes and dreams? *To the waters and the wild.*

What if nothing is wasted? What if there's a blue flame on our inner country that we can conjure with the fire of courage in our hearts, to melt our perceived failures down and turn them into something else?

The importance of our desire to create, without knowing how to access the world of our imaginations, can become overwhelming. We can overthink how much it means to us and end up procrastinating instead of creating. Our minds can take us far from where we need to be, in our bodies, accompanying ourselves and our creative instinct. The way we come back to ourselves, come back to our creativity, is a tool we already possess in our minds: the ability to be present.

FAILURE + NOTHING IS WASTED PROVOCATIONS

What if your perceived failures were fairy doors to the first, necessary, beautiful steps on the road to finding more creative joy in your life?

How would it feel to embrace and celebrate imperfection in your creativity as part of learning and growing?

What if it was impossible to fail because your central motivation to create was for the pure joy and pleasure of it?

What hidden/discarded Ideas in your scrap pot might you melt down and turn into something else?

Do you have any 'shitty' ideas that you could, pardon the pun, dung-beetle-the-shit-out-of and turn into a beautiful, repurposed idea?

4

Procrastination + Presence: An Overgrown Path

I've often been asked if writing *The Lost Flowers of Alice Hart* was cathartic, healing or therapeutic, and I've always found it tricky to give a straight answer. It was all those things. Also euphoric, freeing, moving, harrowing, challenging and terrifying. And, often, writing that book really, really, really pissed me off, a feeling that was compounded at the time by my inability to understand it, or to come to grips with why writing was so hard. I was about to learn the meaning of Gloria Steinem's famous phrase 'The truth will set you free, but first it will piss you off.'

Every day that I showed up at my desk in Manchester to write, I grappled with why it felt as agonising and impossible as pulling teeth. Even after the death in my family jolted me out of fear's grip and I learned that I could feel afraid but write anyway, there were still countless days when I tried to write but felt torn in two. I wanted to write, but I couldn't write. When I sat down to write, my imagination – that sense of going inwards to ideas, lush, rich and flowing – seemed so far away, hidden from view.

Days passed that way. I couldn't draw anything from my mind or heart onto paper. I got fidgety. Started cleaning my office instead. Which led to cleaning out the fridge downstairs. Then the bathroom cabinets. I even took on the Useless Shit Drawer, that one we all have in the kitchen where the detritus from our lives goes to die. When volunteers knocked on the door asking for donations, I struck up long conversations. Same with the Fish Man, some bloke who regularly went door to door in Manchester selling fresh fish. I got to know our local postie so well we were on first-name terms. Andy. I loved him – he never tried to hide the shock on his face when he knocked on the door to deliver my mail at two in the afternoon and I was in my bathrobe with a pen holding my hair up, looking like an approximation of the zombie emoji. 'Going well today, then?' he'd ask me with a grin as he handed over the post. Of course, he'd heard pretty much my entire life story and knew I was trying to write my first novel. He always made me laugh.

My other procrastination vice, which we all know too well, was the slippery slope of the internet. The easiest way to numb myself, tap out and lose hours of the day was down the sinkhole of any social media app, online shopping website or streaming service. I'd never experienced procrastination like it. And it distressed the hell out of me. I figured I'd done my part of the deal – shown up at my desk – but my brain had pulled up stumps and shut down. What the fuck was wrong with me?

After a few months of continuing this way, I couldn't stand how it felt, holding all these emotions in my body like a dam ready to burst. I had jitters in my limbs; I needed to move.

Austin Kleon's *Steal Like an Artist* had a permanent place on my desk: I flicked to my favourite section, which had inspired me to create my own analogue and digital desks. 'You need to find a way to bring your body into your work. Our nerves aren't a one-way street – our bodies can tell our brains as much as our brains tell our bodies.' What was my body telling me there in my office, feeling such deep resistance to what I was trying to do? Whatever it was, I knew that staying there, feeling physically full of yearning and desire at the same time as repulsion and resistance, wasn't giving me the answer. Neither was cleaning, chatting or searching the internet. I needed a different response. So, one day I laced up my running shoes. And that's when I learned that running can also be writing.

A common misconception about procrastination is that it's related to laziness – that we put off doing what we want to do because we just can't be bothered. Behavioural research says it's more complex than that.

James Clear, author of *Atomic Habits: An Easy and Proven Way to Build Good Habits and Break Bad Ones*, writes about a pattern in human behaviour called 'time inconsistency'. It explains what's happening in our minds when we procrastinate, and the problematic power of valuing instant gratification over future rewards. A way to understand how 'time inconsistency' works is to imagine that we are, in any given moment, two selves: 'Present Self' and 'Future Self'. When we set goals for ourselves – like, say, painting a portrait, writing a novel, composing and recording a song, rehearsing a performance or planting a veggie garden – we're effectively planning for something that our Future Self will accomplish and be rewarded by, which we also understand will shape our lives in the future. When we consider our Future Self, it's easy for our minds to understand the value of 'taking actions with long-term benefits'. Our Future Self appreciates long-term rewards.

And what about our Present Self? Does it appreciate long-term rewards? Not so much. Our Present Self wants rewards now, in the present. Now, now, now. (An image of Veruca Salt demanding a golden goose egg comes to mind – 'I want it now!')

While our Future Self is a goal-setter, it's our Present Self that has the power to act. This is where the conflict between our two selves lies. When faced with making decisions that inform the actions we take, our minds are by default in Present Self mode. And Present Self really, really *loooooooves* instant gratification instead of having to wait and do the work for a future payoff. (It's like a toddler being offered one doughnut now or a box of doughnuts next week. Most times, the answer will be 'Gimme the doughnut immediately!')

This push and pull between our two selves – Present and Future – and between making choices that give us instant reward versus future reward is what's at the root of procrastination, James Clear argues. Rather than it being a question of overcoming laziness, what's happening when we procrastinate is that we are struggling to regulate our impulses and emotions.

Behind our house in Manchester is a paved path that once was a train line. Now it's used by cyclists, runners, walkers and families. Continuing for kilometres in either direction, it connects suburbs of differing socioeconomic backgrounds, and winds through groves of cherry blossom, silver birch and beech trees. There are long stretches where the path is lined by purple buddleia, moon-flower vines, rampant ivy and elderflower shrubs, and occasional meadows full of wildflowers that are thick with lemon butterflies in the spring. After I left my desk and laced up my shoes, I went to this path and started to run. In the middle of Manchester, the world's first industrial city, this path through flourishing, rolling woodlands and flowering fields reminded me that not everything is always as it might seem. Maybe the procrastination I felt at my desk wasn't necessarily an indication that I couldn't do it, that I couldn't write my novel. Maybe the reason I was so pissed off was about something more than that. Something deeper. Truer.

Day after day, week after week, I returned to run along that path behind our house. To keep running against the terrible resistance I felt surge through me every time I sat at my writing desk. To keep listening to what my body might have to tell me. The main thing I gradually came to understand and trust, after weeks of running, was a quiet yet insistent belief that I should not take the resistance I felt at my desk as an indication to give up on Alice Hart, or myself. I kept writing in whatever little fits and spurts I could.

But continuing to experience such an ongoing and strong resistance to writing Alice's story, and procrastinating my way through day after day, I started to despair. So I kept running. Kept thinking about why writing felt so hard. One foot in front of the other. Eyes fixed on the path ahead. Step by step. In wind, rain, under grey skies or, well, less grey skies. One breath in, one breath out. I kept running.

At most, I usually ran along the path for about four kilometres before I turned and ran home. I continued running that way for a few months until one beautiful summer's day, a rarity in Manchester, I was so full of endorphins and the joy of feeling the sun on my skin that I ran all the way to the path's end, where I came upon something surprising and glorious: the Manchester Donkey Sanctuary.

I went into the grounds, spent some time watching the donkeys grazing, said hello to the ones that came near me. After that day, I kept running, from home to the Donkey Sanctuary and back again. I loved hearing their braying in the distance.

After months of showing up at my desk to write and writing very little, and just about choking on how pissed off I was about my inability to stop procrastinating, one day I quite literally ran myself into an epiphany.

That day, full of anguish, I went out for a run as usual, but I pushed it too hard: I ran without being properly warmed up and sprained a muscle in my hip. I limped home, furious with myself for not being more gentle or wise with my body.

As I hobbled towards my front door, something that had been dry and unyielding cracked open inside me. Out the truth flowed and flooded through me. An understanding of what had been so distressing me for so long at my desk.

I was trying to force myself to write about something that my mind perceived as dangerous – experiencing and living with violence. I finally understood: every time I'd tried to write, unresolved post-traumatic stress in my mind was coming up against an instinctive wish for instant gratification. The result was a stalemate. The sensation of a physical blockage. The sense of nothingness. That was why it was so much easier to clean out a cupboard or vacuum the house than try to write in that state.

I limped inside my house and ran myself an Epsom salts bath. I didn't feel like I was crying, but my eyes were nevertheless weeping. *The truth will set you free, but first it will piss you off.*

I reflected on my running training. When I first started running the path behind our house, I took slow, measured steps and aimed to run short distances to allow my body to get used to it and the Manchester weather, which, coming from the heat of the Australian desert and coast, I wasn't used to. But when I sat down at my writing desk, the steps I was aiming to take were way too big. *Write Chapter 6*, I'd have on my to-do list. My brain shrivelled in response. It was too much, too fast, too soon.

I decided to try writing my novel by taking smaller steps towards smaller goals. I didn't realise it then, but this new process I was intuitively setting up for myself to try to learn how to write well, with a sense of ease rather than stress, was not so different at all from how the donkeys in the sanctuary nearby were learning too.

In the world of donkey rehabilitation and training, the best way to help a donkey learn, says Ben Hart, senior lead in behaviour and human behaviour change at the Donkey Sanctuary UK, is to use the process of shaping behaviour. Shaping, Hart explains, is the process of breaking down a desired behaviour – like having a calm donkey for a safe farrier visit – into small steps or learning blocks, and then adding them together in a sequence, through training, leading to the desired outcome.

Humans inherently know how to shape behaviour, Hart says. We all instinctively know we need to walk before we can run, and we learned to crawl before we could walk. Shaping behaviour is integral for learning in both animals and humans.

But, as humans, we're not great at shaping behaviour when we focus too much on our anticipated outcome and want to reach it as quickly as possible. Caught up in our enthusiasm to learn or achieve something new, Hart says, 'we make our learning steps too big', not realising that when the steps in our learning process are beyond our ability to achieve, we've inadvertently made learning harder for ourselves.

Donkeys are no different. For Hart, the saying 'Don't fear small steps, fear standing still' lies at the heart of his work. The challenge of good shaping, Hart says, is how small to make the steps. 'The smaller you make the steps the easier and safer training becomes.'

Another fundamental part of implementing shaping behaviour in Hart's work with donkeys is a written plan outlining every step, then breaking each step down into detail and sequential order. Having a written plan is also a powerful way, Hart says, to avoid 'going to the problem to solve the problem'. If he's having an issue with picking up a donkey's feet, it might seem logical and easy to try to solve that problem by just trying to pick up the donkey's foot. This more likely than not leads to stressing the donkey and causing kicking. But a written shaping plan to pick up the donkey's feet breaks the process down into such small steps that both the donkey and the human trainer can avoid distress and are kept safe. An example of a small starting step might be to have the donkey stand calmly with their human trainer by their shoulder. Then there might be five smaller steps that need to be completed before the trainer can successfully pick up the donkey's foot.

The power of shaping behaviour and the power of having small steps written down in a well-thought-through plan is that the smaller Hart makes the steps, the faster the donkey will learn. If he makes learning logical and easy for the donkey, with the steps so small that the donkey can't fail, the animal is calmer, quicker and more responsive.

Although I'd realised what my problem was, going to my desk still felt terrifying – to face the page, to attempt to create. I filled my fountain pens with fresh ink. Organised my notebooks. Scrolled through social media for distraction, which only filled my mind with noise and caused my focus to fracture. A temptation rose in me to put on a load of washing, to water my plants, to sort through my spice rack and go for a walk to the supermarket because I needed paprika. I took a deep, steadying breath. Called to mind the affirmations I focused on when I was out on a run. *One foot in front of the other. Keep breathing. Get out of your head and trust your body, you know the way.*

I opened my Word document to Alice Hart's story. Saw her face in my mind. Something pulled in my heart. The knowledge, the knowing, that she couldn't exist without me. My fingers hovered over my keyboard.

My running routine had taught me that there was immeasurable power to be found in taking things one step at a time, and that had eventually led to me hitting my stride. I experientially knew this was true beyond running from the work I'd done in therapy and the effort I'd put into recovering from post-traumatic stress. First one step, then another. It's how I walked myself through grief and trauma into making a new life.

My fingers hovered. *You know how to do this*, I told myself. *Little steps.*

I didn't start writing straight away. Instead, I started typing a list. My first step was setting myself tiny, manageable steps instead of something broad and overwhelming like *Write Chapter 6.*

On some days, my to-do lists included the smallest and most obvious steps, like *Take shower. Brush teeth. Get dressed.* Ticking them off my list gave me a dopamine rush that propelled me to my writing desk. Once I got there, instead of expecting myself to write tens of thousands of brilliant words in perfectly constructed sentences, I continued to set small and achievable steps for myself. *Write the opening paragraph of Alice's first morning at Thornfield.* Immediately, I could smell Candy's cooking wafting up the stairs to Alice's bedroom in the bell tower. I could hear the magpies warbling from the flower fields, and the tinkle of Harry's collar as he moved on the floor beside Alice's bed. Little steps revealed a path beneath my feet. Inwards, to my inner country of imagination. Step by step by step.

Breaking my writing down into these small, achievable steps led me through the gauntlet of writing a novel, which in its entirety had been too much for me, too overwhelming, too challenging. Word after word, I wrote a sentence, which led into a paragraph. The motivation I felt from seeing a paragraph written in my notebook or on my screen enabled me to take another little step towards continuing to put Alice's story on paper. The more I wrote, the more I learned that taking small steps was an effective way to regulate my emotional reaction to writing. My Present Self felt rewarded. That sense of accomplishment drove me on. The more muscle I built up around writing, the more I began to feel the love and joy of doing it return to me.

It was through that love and joy that I began to feel present, in my body, when I wrote. I began to settle at my desk. And I began to create rituals around my writing process that helped me to stay with myself, moment to moment, while I was writing. I would light a candle, say a silent prayer of thanks and surrender, arrange a vase of flowers for myself at my desk, paint my fingernails a particular colour depending on the scene I was writing, listen to music, and practise yoga moves to stretch and warm up my body before I started working. Those rituals cleared the path beneath my feet and let the sunlight in; I learned to follow the path, step by step, away from fear-based procrastination, into joy-based presence. Into the world of my imagination.

When it comes to procrastination, James Clear writes, we can't rely on future rewards to motivate our Present Self. Instead, we must find ways to bring those future rewards into the present moment, where we make decisions and act. Behavioural psychology agrees that the line between procrastination and taking action is a boiling point, where the pain of procrastinating and/or the pressure of what we're putting off doing becomes so intense that it forces us to act. As soon as we have crossed the line between procrastinating and action, Clear says, all the pain, stress and anguish that we've been feeling, that caused us to reach that boiling point, instantly begins to subside. He writes, 'Being in the middle of procrastination is often more painful than being in the middle of doing the work … The guilt, shame, and anxiety you feel while procrastinating are usually worse than the effort and energy you have to put in while you're working. The problem is not *doing* the work, it's *starting* the work.' If we want to stop procrastinating, Clear advises, we need to make it as easy

Holly in a park off the path behind her house in Manchester

as possible for our Present Self to get started on the work, and trust that motivation and momentum will come after we begin.

It feels likely to me that if you're reading this book, the siren call of procrastination is not unknown to you. You're familiar with going to your desk – dance floor, workbench, kitchen counter, garden, design software, guitar – and showing up. You're ready to create. And then … nothing. You freeze. Creativity eludes you. So you go on Instagram, make a phone call, decide you really should sweep up the leaves in your backyard … You may not be managing trauma like me, but you're managing something. We all are. Maybe a sense of guilt that you're taking time away from family or friends for your creative work. A sense that you're somehow being 'indulgent' or fanciful or deluding yourself for wanting to create. Or maybe you recall a harshly critical comment from a friend when you confided in them what you're creating or wanting to create … Whatever it is – discomfort, guilt or shame – it is fuelling your procrastination. As it does for all of us.

The truth is that creating – making something out of nothing – is hard. But, when it comes to our creativity, what if we could learn another way to manage procrastination so that it's not pain that propels us finally into action, but joy? What if practising shaping behaviour in ourselves – by making and listing small, achievable steps that we can take towards whatever it is we want to create – is an effective way to do just that? To motivate our present selves. To make the process rewarding *and* joyful. To reduce the fear of starting so we can just get the fuck out of our own way and see the ground, the path, beneath our feet?

What if the very thing about creativity that we love – that is, the joy it brings us to engage in it – is the way forward?

While writing this chapter, I call Libby. We've made a date to talk about procrastination and creativity. I ask Libs what creativity means to her.

'It's how I come out of my head and into my body,' she says, smiling. 'Creativity happens when my imagination and my senses come together. I create when I want to feel and give myself joy.' She tells me that over the past twenty years she's learned to prioritise making time for creativity in her day-to-day life because the joy she gets from being creative develops and restores her resilience. Libs, like all of us in our modern lives, is busy. She has a demanding job, a big family and is a meditation practitioner, which requires writing, recording and producing her meditations in her own time.

I ask how she engages with creativity each day.

'Making an oil blend for the diffuser I have going in the office, having open-hearted conversations, cooking a meal, putting together the colours in my outfits and accessories for the day, painting with watercolours, rearranging the house and my plants, designing spreadsheets. You know how I love a spreadsheet.'

I do know. This is the woman who voluntarily made spreadsheets to help me pack my suitcases every year when I came home from the UK to Australia for Christmas. I hated packing so much that some years I was still furiously throwing things into a suitcase on the morning of my flight. Libby's spreadsheets had colour-coding, weather forecasts for the different places I would be travelling to within Australia and coordinated wardrobe choices (because a best friend knows your wardrobe that well). The thought of opening Excel makes my soul dry up. But for Libs the idea of making a spreadsheet brings untold creative joy.

'Tell me about procrastination,' I say. We both sigh.

'The biggest thing I've figured out when I feel like I'm procrastinating is to first check in with myself with a no-bullshit question,' she says. I mention my Bullshit-o-Meter, which Libby has known about for years. She laughs and nods.

'I ask myself, "No bullshit, Libby, are you lying on the couch watching re-runs of *Grand Designs* because you're procrastinating and scared of creating, or do you just need rest?" If I need rest, I stay on the couch, because I know it's what I truly need. But if I get any whiff of my own bullshit, I get up off the couch and work with myself to move through fear so I can start to create and do what I really want to be doing.'

I ask what she thinks her procrastination habit stems from.

'The fear of being seen and heard. Of trying and failing. The fear of being irrelevant. Of being too much.'

In the two decades we've known the details of each other's lives so intimately, we've never had this exact conversation. Both of us choke up. We're never as alone or strange as we think we are.

'So how do you start,' I ask, 'when starting is so painful and scary?'

Libby says she's learned enough about herself to know what her imagination responds to, which is creating a space that engages and nourishes her senses. When she's procrastinating and caught in either the red-hot rage or cold, numbing fear of it, she follows little steps and rituals she knows will take her inwards. Libby uses things like music, incense, brewing tea, adjusting the lighting in her room and gathering tactile materials to create a cocoon for her creativity where, whether she's raging or numb from procrastination, she can still soften. She finds refuge in her surroundings, a sense of safety, which allows her to become present in herself, within her body.

'Does it always work?' I ask. 'Taking those little steps and following rituals to meet procrastination so you can just start?'

She pauses as she considers her answer. 'I might not always end up writing a meditation I'm happy with or painting something that feels right, but I've shown up, and honoured my urge to create. I've learned that honouring the part of me that's asking to make something, giving myself the time and space I need to do that, matters more to me than whatever it is I end up creating. That's the joy. Showing up for my creativity, not stuffing it away out of fear or shame.'

In an interview on Brené Brown's podcast *Unlocking Us*, Edith Eger, psychologist, author and Holocaust survivor, talks about how she defines love. To her, love is a four-letter word: T-I-M-E. Our time is the biggest gift we can give, she explains. When we make time for ourselves and each other, we feel something very powerful: we feel worthy.

Giving our time to our creativity, so we can go inwards and create from our inner country, is no different from making time and space for the people we love.

No less an act of love. No less worthy.

In the final pages of my second novel, *The Seven Skins of Esther Wilding*, Esther has a conversation with a special friend she's made in the Faroe Islands, who tells her about the mystery of the annual monarch butterfly migration from northeastern North America to the forests of central Mexico, a distance of some four thousand kilometres.

It puzzled scientists for years: why do monarchs take a sudden eastward turn at a specific point over Lake Superior year after year? Doing so makes the already tough journey even harder. They could just fly directly south, saving themselves huge difficulty. Yet every year at this specific point in their migration they turn

Spend time doing what you love.

east, fly for a while, and then veer south. No one could figure it out until geologists and biologists finally connected their research: thousands of years ago, the theory goes, a mountain once rose from the lake at the exact point where the butterflies turned east. This geological memory has been inherited by generations of offspring who have never seen the mountain but still fly out of their way to avoid it. No one knows how they pass on this knowledge. Just that they do, and it shapes the course of their lifespan.

Consider this: a monarch butterfly weighs less than half a gram. But with its tiny wings, it travel thousands of kilometres, around invisible mountains, following an ancient path, towards warmer days.

We all have a path inwards, intuitively known to us. It might be overgrown with decades of fears, all those vines and thorns, but it's still there, in you and me. We can still follow it back into places we thought were lost to us. *We, who have lived in it, and loved it, and left it … can Never-Never rest away from it.*

If the path is hidden from you, know it's there. Waiting for you to uncover it. Which you can do by giving your creativity the gift of your T-I-M-E.

And L-O-V-E.

And by practising whatever rituals bring you joy and aid you in acting from joy as your source instead of intense fear or pain.

Small steps, one in front of the other, take us through the vines and thorns to the path. We know the way to our inner country. Our Present Selves can accept who we are in any moment, create from that place just as we are, and take care of the creativity of our Future Selves. In a year's time, you might find yourself wishing you'd taken your first small step today.

Truth: you are allowed to make time to do what you love. Rage against falling through the floor of your own life. This is your ground to stand on. To till. To flourish. Your inner critic might get on a loudhailer with the message that creativity is for everyone else but you. But your inner critic just hasn't realised yet that it has an equal: your inner fan.

PROCRASTINATION + PRESENCE PROVOCATIONS

How can you prioritise more time for creativity in your life?

If you get distracted, what rituals might help bring you back to your body and reaffirm your intention to give your creativity time?

What tiny steps might make the creative process easier? Can you make a shaping plan of tiny steps to identify and outline your creative process?

What overgrown paths into your imagination might these tiny steps help you rediscover?

How might your Future Self feel to know that your Present Self honoured and fulfilled your desire to build more creative space in your life?

What creative joy might be waiting for you if you stop putting off taking those first tiny steps?

5

Inner Critic + Inner Fan: Stay Gold

In 1987, when I was about seven years old, one of my reasons to visit my cousins was to get access to their toys. Particularly their My Little Pony collection. Seeing how enamoured I became of the pastel ponies, my mum surprised me one day with one of my own: Starshine. We were instant best friends.

While I unquestionably loved Starshine's rainbow mane, wings and golden-star-embossed rump, it was her story and spirit that made me feel seen. I remember my awe as I read, in the booklet that came with the toy, about the secret, magical adventure Starshine bravely had, all by herself.

Thanks to fellow *My Little Pony* fans on the internet, I've rediscovered Starshine's story through a photo of the original 1980s packaging. It details the solo adventure Starshine had one rainy day when she wanted to have some fun. With help from rainbow light in the dark, stormy sky, Starshine travelled up into an enchanted land, where she played with the Milky Way, the moon and other stars.

I was an only child then, and Starshine's lone journey to seek her own fun and excitement was something I recognised from the hours I spent playing behind the flowering curtain of *Bauhinia galpinii* in our garden, or climbing the bottlebrush tree, or sitting under the giant fronds of Mum's ferns. We lived a block from the Pacific Ocean on Bundjalung Country then; I understood how Starshine felt visiting enchanting lands because of all the hours I spent collecting treasures along the shore – native hibiscus, seed pods, shells, seaweed – while I talked to the vast and ever-changing sea. I understood how magical a beam of enchanting light could be from the countless days of my childhood I spent walking the green trails through our nearest national park, on Yugambeh Country, where the sunlight turned gold, violet and emerald as it shone through the gnarled, moss- and lichen-covered branches of thousand-year-old Antarctic beech trees. I knew how Starshine felt, looking at the Milky Way and talking to the stars. I did the same thing at night.

Holly, around five years old, treasure-hunting by the sea, Bundjalung Country

Whenever I played with Starshine, something wondrous happened: I discovered new worlds inside myself. I realise now that Starshine was one of the first keepers of my inner country (along with Falkor and Artax from *The Neverending Story*, and Tinkerbell from *Peter Pan*). She and her fellow ponies and all their stories became representations of my imagination and all the imagined lives and worlds in which I had adventures. Full of rainbows and possibility. Full of hope and joy, fun and excitement, safety and belonging.

But as I matured and went through the self-consciousness of adolescence and the angst of my early twenties, it wasn't so easy to access my imagination in the same innocent way. My inner critic reared up and the happy little ponies of my young imagination changed into wild, unpredictable horses with hard hooves and hostile behaviour that trampled through my mind. My imagination became a fraught, difficult place.

When I was trying to piece my life together after leaving the desert, my inner critic was in one of its most unruly and strongest periods – a rageful, stampeding brumby. That's when I made the decision to move alone to the UK to follow my dream of becoming a writer.

The term 'inner critic' is a popular name for the negative running commentary we all have in our minds, an inner dialogue that often feels like it's ever ready to criticise every aspect of our behaviour and value. It can be judgemental or harsh, and sometimes outright cruel. The power and danger of listening to the belittling commentary of our inner critic is that we can unconsciously accept this deeply negative way of thinking about ourselves as Truth. Believing this Truth keeps us small.

Some of my inner critic's greatest hits:

You're not smart enough to write a whole novel. There's no point in trying, because you're only going to find out what you already fear to be true: you're not good enough to write a good book.

You're not brave enough to handle ever sharing your creative work with anyone. You're only going to make a fool of yourself if you do that.

Who do you think you are, making time to write stories? As if that's a valuable way to spend your time when there are so many other things to do and so many other people are relying on you?

It's selfish of you to want to create, to take up space with your creativity. You think everyone in the world gets the luxury of being able to write stories? What makes you so special?

Prioritising your joy and creativity is irresponsible, insensitive and deeply self-absorbed when so many others are suffering. You're not worthy of creating. Don't try anything new.

You might think you're a writer, but what if you're a one-trick pony? Stick to what you know. What you know is safe.

For decades I listened to this kind of commentary from my inner critic. I carried these thoughts as Truth in my body, against my body. The weight of it hurt and kept me small.

Psychotherapist Lauren Canonico says many of her clients realise that they're harshly self-critical, but what they're less aware of are the impossibly high standards they've set and where those standards come from. 'Most people don't know how they came to feel the way they do about themselves,' she explains.

One way of understanding and disassembling the vice-like grip our inner critic has on our lives is to become aware of its origins. Psychotherapist Christina Cruz, who specialises in working with people suffering from anxiety, perfectionism and depression, suggests the inner critic originates from early experiences with primary caregivers. How these figures relate to us and perceive us in the world is what we internalise. 'Their voice and perceptions of us become our voice and become how we relate to ourselves. Because primary caregivers have such a strong role in our lives, it is difficult to develop a sense of self outside of what others believe us to be.'

Figures of authority can also affect how we perceive and relate to ourselves, and our creativity. That aunt or uncle or cousin at a family birthday gathering who tells us we're no good at singing after we've just belted out a joyous rendition of 'Happy Birthday'. Or the friend who scoffs when we share that we've decided to make time to prioritise our desire to paint, cook, dance, draw, garden or learn a new language.

When we dare to create, we're daring to be vulnerable, and when we're vulnerable, we can be porous. If we're not mindful, external criticisms can become our own. As Lauren Canonico explains, not only do we internalise how these figures in our lives relate to and perceive us – our creativity – in the world, but we also internalise their feelings and criticisms of themselves, and 'hold ourselves to those same standards'.

Our inner critics can be further fed by the societal messaging we receive about ourselves and how we express our creativity. The world repeatedly tells us who we are based on our appearance, race, culture, religion, sexual orientation, financial standing … it goes on. And the world judges us – constantly. It can be as subtle as a raised eyebrow from someone you know – 'Oh, you're wearing *that*?' – to shouted slurs from strangers on the street. Everything about us gives the world reasons to judge us. The volume of our laugh. The way we talk or dress. The size and shape of our bodies. The colour of our skin. Our vulnerability and truths. Our confidence. Or lack thereof. The boundaries we set. The ones we don't. All this external feedback feeds the critic within. As Lauren Canonico says, these messages 'seemingly confirm the inner critic's negative stance and strengthen it even further'. Fuelled by the fear that we are not good enough, or worthy, our inner critic continuously looks for evidence to prove our not-enoughness and worthlessness.

Is it any surprise that when it comes to our creativity – which is all about opening ourselves up and responding to what moves us – our inner critic is deeply threatened? That it reacts to that threat by rearing up and charging with everything it's got to trample our desire to create? In effect, Starshine gets flattened by stampeding brumbies.

Okay. Deep breath. Here's the uplift: we can change our relationship with our inner critic because we can change the relationship we have with ourselves. It's hard, and it can take lifelong practice. Nevertheless. Despite how constant and persistent our inner critic is, we *still* have the power to reject its feedback as Truth. In any given moment, on any given day of our lives, we can begin to change how we respond to our inner critic.

I arrived in England on a one-way ticket with two duffel bags and a wine box of books to my name. A dear friend I'll call James, then living in London, picked me up from Heathrow. After a brief stay in his Soho flat, James drove me north to the red-brick city that would become my home, where I knew no one.

Everything was new, daunting and unfamiliar. I tried to feel excitement about my fresh start. But my inner critic had me in its grip. *What have you done? Moving here to write? Do you know how small the odds are that this is going to work out for you? This is ridiculous. You can't do this. You're going to fall into a hole here.*

The next day, James helped me move into my student accommodation. By afternoon I was settled, with nothing left to do but wait for postgraduate orientation to start. James hugged me goodbye. I stood in the street and watched his tail-lights shrink from view. The chill of the September air went through my bones. *It's only a matter of time before you admit this was a massive fuck-up and you scurry home with your tail between your legs.* I took a shaky breath.

Two days later, after hours of orientation lectures and student information sessions, I wasn't the twenty-nine-year-old, glowing, duck-to-water postgraduate student I'd dreamed I might be. I was feverish and shaky; I didn't understand how to dress in my new climate (I either had too many or too few layers on) and my energy was depleted. I thought about leaving the lecture theatre early. But the last orientation talk of the day interested me: it was about a charity in Manchester called the International Society, which encouraged global friendship and cultural diversity. I stayed put. The talk started. A smiling man walked onto the stage looking like Shaggy from *Scooby Doo*. He introduced himself as Sam. Then he regaled us with hilarious and heart-warming stories about students just like me who had made cross-cultural friendships and had life-changing experiences through the International Society. Suddenly the whole lecture theatre was alive and laughing, engaged by Sam's storytelling. For the first time since I'd arrived, I felt hopeful.

Afterwards, feeling inspired, I went to the International Society to become a member. I recognised Sam sitting in the foyer and blurted out something about enjoying his talk. He smiled and thanked me. There was kindness and gentleness in his eyes. He asked if my accent was Australian. After I said yes, he told me he missed his younger brother, who was living in Melbourne. When he asked me where in Australia I came from, I surprised myself by talking candidly about the desert, something I didn't often do then. Sam invited me to have lunch the following week so we could keep talking. I mumbled yes, rushed away, and then spent days freaking out about it. I convinced myself I wouldn't have lunch with him, even as I walked into the café where we'd agreed to meet. The conversation we started that uncharacteristically sunny afternoon has been ongoing now for nearly fourteen years.

On my fourth day in Manchester, when I least expected it and had no reason to trust, I met the kindest human I've ever known. My inner critic had me so convinced to expect the worst of myself in the UK. Meeting Sam, letting myself see him, and letting myself be seen by him, was so unlikely. I wasn't prepared in any way to expect the best from my lone journey to England. Nonetheless, it happened.

I'm sure there are countless things I haven't made or created because my inner critic told me I couldn't and shouldn't. Unknown opportunities that I've been too scared to look for, or invitations that I've felt unworthy of accepting. Moments I haven't lived, wonders, connections and joys I haven't felt. Numerous times when listening to my inner critic and staying small was easier than betting on myself, taking a risk and saying, *I can*.

Being locked out of our creativity, our inner country, our selves, *by ourselves* can be incredibly painful. But being dogged by our inner critic can also teach us where our threshold is, when enough of being controlled by that negative, cruel commentary is enough. Without all the years when I was too scared to try to write anything, I wouldn't have learned how full of smoke and mirrors my inner critic is, and, bewilderingly, I would never have learned that, at its heart, my inner critic actually wants me to grow, and flourish, and succeed. It just wants me to do that in a way that doesn't involve any risk whatsoever.

A question: what if our inner critic is trying to help? What if our inner critic is trying to protect us from feeling the pain of rejection, failure and harm? It's almost laughable, I know, to think that our inner critic has good intentions. If that's the case, I've countless times wondered, why is the commentary of our inner critic so fucking mean? The answer is a simple one: our inner critic stems from fear, shame and scarcity. When we fight back, it can seem to grow stronger and louder, powered up by aggression and resistance. Something our inner critic will never tell us: what it needs most is compassion and love.

Another question: what if our inner critic is at its strongest when it's reacting to the things that are most important to us?

Follow-on questions: what would happen to the power of our inner critic if we treated it like a signal, like a gauge to help us better understand our relationship with creativity? What if we acknowledged, *Oooof, this recipe or painting or short story or novel or poem or knitting or sheet music must really matter to me if my inner critic is going so haywire about it. I must be terrified of losing it, I must really want it. How can I move more towards it because it's what I really want, rather than fearing it because it's what I really want?*

From our first conversation, being around Sam's calm, grounded energy felt infectious. When I told him I'd moved to England to follow my dream of becoming a writer, my face flamed with embarrassment about how foolish I sounded. But Sam's eyes lit up. He asked me more about my writing. I told him how I'd dreamed of becoming a writer as a kid, with my head full of stories and a hunger for adventure. A sense of recognition registered on Sam's face. When I pressed him about it, he told me he'd recently bought a derelict schoolhouse in a mountain village in ex-communist Bulgaria to help a Bulgarian friend with her dream of regenerating the village. Through the process he'd travelled to Bulgaria, shared meaningful, joyous connections with new friends, created magical memories and felt his life expanding in countless enriching ways. It made my head spin to hear him talk that way about taking risks for joy.

I just checked my emails – this is from the second email Sam ever sent to me, after that first lunch meeting:

> I have no idea what you are like as a writer, but I do know that when I bought the derelict school people surrounded me with negative comments and said things like 'villages die', 'you're crazy and you're throwing your money into a black hole'. Looking back, I gained loads of strength from it and learnt to follow the stars that appear.
>
> Even if none of it works out, I have had the most amazing journey and wouldn't change a thing.
>
> So I say … you're amazing to follow your dream.
>
> Head for the stars :)

Reading Sam's email was freeing. I didn't have to be in England to become a writing 'success'; I could be there to have fun, experience joy and give meaning to my life.

The more time I spent getting to know Sam, the more I learned and understood that seeing the good in people was inherent to him. I noticed it in his interactions with others. Confusingly, it seemed like he saw goodness in me too.

After a while, it seemed like Sam's acceptance and belief were starting to rub off on me. My mindset slowly became lighter, softer, gentler, more encouraging and self-soothing. My inner critic was very much still there, but there was something else rising to meet it: an equal, opposite energy in me. Was self-belief something I could catch from Sam? Ed Batista, an executive coach, writes that emotions are literally contagious – we sense them in others, pick them up and pass them on. Being in Sam's regular company was a revelatory lesson for me. (So, next time you're tempted to condemn yourself for having no self-esteem or for feeling flat and lacklustre, make sure you're not just surrounded by arseholes.)

Basking in Sam's company – his acknowledgement and acceptance of who I showed him I was – I began to see myself through his eyes and to internalise some of his belief in me. I started to see for myself the possibility of all I was becoming. I was more than what had happened to me. My inner critic had gone unchecked for so long without any counterbalance, but meeting Sam at that juncture in my life and allowing myself to engage in our developing friendship, and then ongoing relationship, was a tipping point. For the first time in a long time, I could see clearly: I'd been bold with my decision-making and my life, even though I'd been absolutely terrified every step of the way. Maybe there was more to me than my inner critic told me there was.

Sam didn't save me. He didn't complete me. He didn't fix me. He met me where I was, as I was, with kindness, respect, belief, joy and inspiration. The power of allowing myself to believe I was worthy of that respect and kindness also allowed me to believe I could do the work I needed to do to remake my life. To own my story. My strength. My courage. And to believe in myself, to know I was a good person, enough as I was, and worthy of my dreams.

Often the inner critic feels a lot like self-doubt. The two, in my experience, are bedfellows. It might be different for you. The slight difference between the two mindsets for me is that self-doubt is specifically connected to how strong or depleted the power of curiosity is in me to stay open and to embrace possibilities with eagerness. Whereas the inner critic is a running commentary in my mind that isn't necessarily connected to possibility or opportunity. It shows up then too, but my inner critic is like a 24/7 news channel, whereas self-doubt isn't always 'on' in the same way.

I reflect on the nature of my inner critic's commentary throughout my adult life. Again, I think of the Libby Test … again I know I wouldn't speak to her or anyone I love this way. I try another test. I imagine attending an art class or a dance class or a painting class for beginners. I play out speaking the commentary of my inner critic to any of my imaginary classmates, complete strangers to me. *You are woefully bad at this. You're just embarrassing yourself. God, do us all a favour and go home.* Do you hear how appalling that sounds? The truth is, I could never utter a word of my inner critic's arsenal to a stranger in response to the beauty of their courage to make something from nothing. Yet this inner dialogue still runs in my mind, constantly on a loop, towards myself. If I don't manage my inner critic, it's still a wild, frightened and unpredictable horse that can lash out. And managing it takes every tool I've ever assembled in my Toolkit of Unfuckable-with Magic: play, self-compassion, nothing is wasted, presence … and my inner fan.

In her widely beloved newsletter, *The Marginalian*, Maria Popova writes, 'To find joy … to find hope … and spark [them] in others, is nothing less than a countercultural act of courage and resistance. To live there is to live enchanted with the underlying wonder of reality.'

An equally powerful way I've found to access that life enchanted, the 'underlying wonder of reality', the realm inside of us – our inner country – where hope and joy and courage and imagination collide, has been by creating and cultivating my inner fan.

Ben Crowe, well known for being Ash Barty's mindset coach, describes our inner fan as a form of role play that uses 'compassionate inquiry' and 'a playful approach' to help us make sense of the stories we're telling ourselves about our lives. In other words, instead of coming to ourselves through a commentary of fear, we come to ourselves through a commentary of fandom: joy, support, positivity. Science writer Michael Bond wrote it beautifully in *The Guardian*: 'To be a fan means many things, but at its heart is an act of love.'

Here's a fact that never lessens in its profundity for me: our inner critic is just a story we tell ourselves. But even being 'just' a story, it's a mighty powerful one. One that we know from experience can negatively shape our behaviour and choices, and ultimately the quality of the lives we live.

Knowing this fact about our inner critic is how we also know that the equal and opposite is true: it's entirely possible for us to tell ourselves another story. One rooted in courage, compassion, love and trust, rather than fear, shame and scarcity. Told from the perspective of our inner fan. Who wants the best for us. Who can be whoever we want them to be. Who allows us to take a compassionate and playful approach with our truest self.

It brings me joy now to tell you about my inner fan.

My inner fan isn't any one person. Or a composite.

It's a feeling. And how my inner fan feels to me can differ depending on what I need.

Sometimes my inner fan is my younger self, walking along the shore of the sea, hands full of strands of seaweed, shells and beach flowers, calling to me, reminding me to be playful and stay curious.

Other times, my inner fan appears in my mind with the energy, charisma and – yes – appearance of Channing Tatum. That's right. Sometimes my inner fan channels how it feels to watch Channing Tatum, whether he's dancing to Ginuwine's song 'Pony' in *Magic Mike* or building a fairy princess castle for his daughter in an Instagram video: absolute joy, wonder and pure delight. Channing Tatum inspires my inner fan when I need to be reminded of how powerful it is to allow ourselves to be unboxed, and to embrace all the different, glorious facets of our creativity. (It would be remiss of me to end this paragraph without acknowledging that Mr Tatum's … wicked grin … might, ahem, also give me a nice feeling.)

I find my inner fan in the way it feels to write a good sentence, the way I felt that day in 2014 when I wrote the first line of *The Lost Flowers of Alice Hart*, and when I wrote one of the last scenes, where everyone gathers at dawn by the sea with pink paper daisies, in *The Seven Skins of Esther Wilding*. My inner fan is the feeling I get when a reader tells me she got a tattoo inspired by something I wrote. Or when I see the joy, love and pride in Sam's face, and my mum and stepdad's faces, when I come out of the office each night and tell them I've written another chapter of this book. Or, as I drift off to sleep some nights, when I know that even if it isn't always comfortable, I'm not living my life bound and small anymore.

However I access the feeling I need from my inner fan, what I'm gathering in, calling up and conjuring are pure and good feelings that steady, inspire, protect and preserve my courage, strength, self-belief, self-compassion and sense of self-value.

Sometimes, I refer to my inner fan by name. Starshine. In honour of the talisman that brought me so much magic and safety in my girlhood.

When I lose or fail, stumble or fall, Starshine reminds me I'm okay, I'm doing my best to show up in this world and I'm enough. Worthy of love, belonging, acceptance and a seat at the table of my life. Starshine reminds me I am allowed to write for joy. I am allowed to create for joy. I am allowed to live and feel joy. In whichever way I choose to express it. And how I do that might be different from how you do it. What a wonderful thing, all the shades and tones and hues of joy in our self-expression. All the stories our inner fans have to tell us about who we are and can be.

One of the ways I honour my inner fan is by returning again and again to the ritual of adornment. Over the past fifteen years, I've cultivated my self-expression through tattoos, accessories, clothing, hairstyles, design, décor, textures and colours. Adorning myself and my spaces this way has been a form of liberating my life from the trauma of violence and control. Adornment is how I've restored my life – joy, colour, desire – from what felt, for so long, like a lifeless state. It's how I regularly practise embodying my creativity – and doffing my hat to Starshine in the process. Adornment has also become a way to resist the fear and scarcity in which my inner critic dwells, and to reject apathy and the seduction of severing myself from feeling. It's my way of preserving a sense of wonder and finding the strength to be present, to feel the discomfort, to stay vulnerable and curious, and to keep showing up, however I can, for myself and others who depend on me.

Expressing myself in this way reminds me that you can feel heavy with grief *and* wear flowers in your hair. You can be struggling with trauma and anxiety *and* find joy in the art of self-decoration. You can feel misunderstood, shut-down *and* simultaneously deeply connected. You can be unsure of every shaky, helpless step, yet feel sure-footed, strong and as if anything is possible. Mess *and* magic. Grief *and* joy. Fear *and* resilience.

This is how I express myself and own my story. You will have your different ways to do the same. We can feel it all, all at once. This is the power in us, and the power of our inner fans.

When it comes to your creativity and your life, your inner fan is yours. Let them show you how much there is about you to love. The joy that you bring to the world around you in seen and unseen ways. Let them cheer for you. When you're faced with the choice of creating, let them have the loudhailer, hear them cry in their best cheerleader voice: WHAT – clap – IF – clap – YOU – clap – CAN?

What?

If?

You?

Can?

But what if you can?

Over the past few years, I've noticed that the more I practise letting myself hear Starshine's commentary, full of compassion for my actions and decisions and behaviour in life, the more empathetic I have become towards my inner critic. Towards the fear, shame and scarcity it dwells in. Towards the love it needs.

It feels radical to empathise with our inner critic. But as humans, we're contradictory and contain multitudes. Plus, it's what Starshine would do.

A quick check-in I have with myself whenever I need to remember the value of my inner fan: Starshine is the mascot of my inner country. Full of possibility, joy, grace, beauty, empathy, curiosity. It's Channing Tatum dancing on air. It's how I adorn and express myself, how I honour the body I live in. It's the voice in my head that tells me, *Stay gold*, with the same conviction I felt as a teen reading *The Outsiders*, moved to tears as Johnny Cade, dying, spoke his now-immortal line: 'Stay gold, Ponyboy.' Most of all, my inner fan is the kid who sat at her writing desk and freely roamed in her imagination and joy, while the hours passed like minutes.

The stories we tell ourselves have the power to transform our lives for the better when we find the strength, courage, love, compassion and trust to listen to them. Developing our inner fan also strengthens our muscles for when we have to deal with our outer critics and find the resilience we need to accompany ourselves, not abandon ourselves, through the pain and discomfort of that criticism.

INNER CRITIC + INNER FAN PROVOCATIONS

Which voices from the past might you carry with you that limit your capacity for creative joy?

What if rather than listening to your inner critic you fired up your inner fan? What would yours be like? How would your inner fan make you feel?

What gold might you find in your inner country? What joy, positivity and courage might you notice in yourself during your experience of looking for that gold?

What might your inner fan encourage you to create from that gold? And from the joy, courage and positivity that led you to discover it?

What might you create if your inner fan is right?

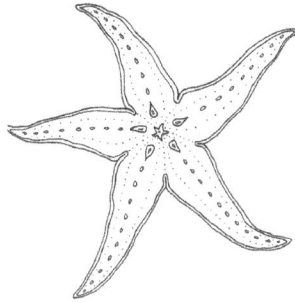

6

Outer Critic + Resilience: We Can Be Starfish

I was around six years old, in Grade Two in primary school, when I encountered my first bully. At the beginning of the school year, I thought we were friends. She came to my house to play; I showed her my desk where I wrote stories, and my Crayola crayon collection. But soon, day after day at school, she started zeroing in on me with a relentless deluge of six-year-old cruelty: name-calling, harassing behaviour and gathering others to join her in ganging up on me.

It was deeply confusing – I didn't know what I'd done to provoke her. We'd never disagreed or fought. She picked on everything about my appearance, from how much she hated my hair and the ribbons Mum tied at the end of my braids, to how much she loathed my face, my eyes, my laugh. She teased me about my schoolbooks that Mum neatly laminated for me. She muttered under her breath when I was asked to read my work aloud in class, to try to throw me off my focus; the fact I'd been asked to share my work particularly incensed her. My desk, stories and creativity I'd previously shared with her became things she mercilessly shamed me about at school. She scoffed at the cut Vegemite sandwiches Mum packed in my lunchbox, teased me about my school uniform that Mum ironed and my leather school shoes Mum bought me from Mathers. She was relentless. I remember she even hated my Raggedy Ann library-book bag Mum sewed for me. You get the idea.

Her bullying was compounded by my sense that it wasn't just an attack on me; she was also mocking my mum. It became so painful for me that I dreaded the weekends ending, when I'd have to go back to school. I was in constant anguish, feeling like I couldn't protect myself or my mum, while wanting to defend us both. It hurt so much that I didn't have any strength or sense of how to stand up to her.

Decades later, the emotional damage she caused is still vivid when I think of her. I realise as I'm writing this that these experiences when I was six years old are among the sources of my lifelong distress and fear around being misunderstood. Who knows what she was going through, the bully? She must have been suffering in her little life – she was only six years old too. I don't remember how or when her bullying stopped; I don't have any memories of her in Grade Three. I assume she must have changed schools.

That experience of being bullied caused one of the first ruptures in my sense of self. The way she perceived and related to me added splinters of self-doubt and self-distrust to my knowledge of who I was. Instead of remembering who I knew myself to be – I was six! – I started believing in the person she told me I was. Later bullying by others compounded these insecurities throughout puberty, adolescence and into my twenties. And thirties. (In my forties now, I try to follow the advice Dame Helen Mirren says she would give to her younger self: say 'fuck off' more and stop being so 'bloody polite'.)

That six-year-old bully started a story I heard over and over again for the next thirty-something years. I was too emotional. Too sensitive. Too sentimental. Away with the fairies. Head in the clouds. Too lost in my own thoughts. Consequently, from a young age, I interpreted my abilities to think and feel deeply and express myself freely as weaknesses I should be ashamed of. So I grew up in many ways warring with myself. Never quite trusting that I belonged in any room I walked into. Never quite knowing if it was okay to speak or join a conversation. Never quite sure if my natural laugh was too loud, or my ideas and thoughts were too emotional to share. I pined to let myself be who I was and for that to be enough. Instead, I looked and listened and checked in constantly with the outside world to tell me who I was, rather than turning inwards to listen to myself.

While the commentary of our inner critic is a story we tell ourselves, outer criticism is the commentary others tell us about how they perceive and relate to who we are. It's a story over which we have no control.

So let's just start this chapter about outer critics with three hard truths:

Being on the receiving end of any outer criticism can feel really fucking awful.

No matter what we do, if we're alive in this world, we're going to be on the receiving end of outer criticism.

Because of this, our creativity will also be subject to outer criticism.

The only way to avoid this happening is to not be in and of the world. To live our lives going out of our way to deny ourselves every single opportunity for connection and growth. As writer and artist Elbert Hubbard wrote, 'To escape criticism: Do nothing, say nothing, be nothing.'

There's an internet meme you might have seen. At the top of the meme is the following text:

THERAPIST: So, where do you think your emotional problems really started?

ME:

Below the meme's text is a still from the film adaptation of Michael Ende's *The Neverending Story,* in which the young warrior, Atreyu, is trying to pull his majestic horse, Artax, free from the Swamp of Sadness. But Artax is stuck in the swamp. Atreyu is deeply distressed, begging Artax to fight off the swamp mud, to fight to be free of it, to fight for his life. But the swamp is heavy and thick. In the moments that follow this frame in the film, Artax loses his fight against the swamp mud and sinks under. It was one of the most distressing and devastating things I'd ever seen in a movie in the first six or seven years of my life. (Any other 1980s babies reading this who relate? Even describing the photo now still fucks me up!)

While writing this chapter I thought of that meme. After I found it on the internet, I was struck again by the power of the scene. Then I realised that it had come to mind because it's a visual depiction of how outer criticism can feel for so many of us – like we're fighting against heavy mud. Made heavier when it's our creativity – something we've created and dared to share – that's being criticised. Or shamed.

Each week during my MA writing class in Manchester, a couple of us submitted a piece of creative writing that was then 'critiqued' by our peers in class, aloud, to the writer's face. When I submitted my work, a fellow student I'll call Boris shocked me with his response. It wasn't just what Boris said in front of the rest of the class to me about my writing – that he found the short story I'd written and submitted to be 'lacking' – but also that Boris told me I'd 'deeply offended' him as a reader with my 'disrespect' in assuming my work was good enough to submit to him and our classmates to read. (When it was Boris's turn to submit, I was not surprised to discover that his short story was a misogynistic tale of a woman having an affair.)

Without having much practice in how to reply constructively to that kind of outer criticism and shaming, no matter how much I might have wanted to find my inner Helen Mirren, I resorted to a response that I knew too well: silence. I was stunned by what I considered to be Boris's sense of entitlement in speaking about my work that way in a class that was meant to foster creativity. In my opinion, his criticism lacked any nuance or value, and reeked instead of plain, cruel bullying. In my stunned state, I copped it on the chin, didn't say a word and kept my head down. Ye gods, how I wish I'd found my Mirren muscles then. But silence was the psychologically safest option available to me at the time.

After class, I sank into the Swamp of Sadness, where I stayed until I found a way to crawl out again. Which was mostly by giving myself time to feel it, talk to friends about it and remind myself I would go back to class the next week.

When we share ourselves through creativity, thereby making ourselves vulnerable, and we receive judgement, criticism and/or shaming in response, it's hard to come back. Painful. Boris's criticism made trying to write a short story again more difficult than it had been the previous time I'd tried. It's this potential effect that outer criticism can have on our creativity that makes it especially threatening: if we haven't developed our Mirren muscles, we risk becoming Artax, and sinking. We might not dare to create again. Maybe we become seduced by the idea that we can avoid the pain of criticism of our creativity if we just stop trying to make something. Easy fix, we might tell ourselves, without realising the pain we are committing ourselves to suffer by letting our creativity go unused. As Brené Brown says, 'Unused creativity is not benign. It metastasizes. It turns into grief, rage, judgment, sorrow, shame.'

The answer? No matter what any Boris thinks of our art, we must still create. For ourselves. For each other. As writer Ocean Vuong says, 'That's how I think of art, [it's] how we are [a] service to one another.'

Here is the part of this book where I say, for the love of all things sacred and holy, please don't ever believe that stopping yourself from creating is the answer. Please. Just fucking create.

There's a reason Nike chose 'Just do it' as its slogan – it's a simple yet power-packed, non-negotiable and profound statement. We can apply it to everything that calls to our heart and is frightening to pursue. It's not always that easy, though, right? To just do it? I know that first-hand. I also understand how infuriating and physically suffocating it can feel to just *not* do it.

The nuts and bolts: Google's English dictionary provided by Oxford Languages defines criticism as 'the expression of disapproval of someone or something on the basis of perceived faults or mistakes'. Apply this definition specifically to our creativity and the things we make for joy, that we might share to offer joy to others, and what most likely happens? *Bam, bam, bam*, red flags around creativity go up and wave for our inner critic to notice: *disapproval, perceived faults, mistakes*. All words that can set off alarms inside ourselves and cause destabilising discomfort around our courage and our creations.

Dipping into cognitive theory for a second, much study has been conducted into why we're more impacted by negative criticism than positive or neutral. Negativity bias, also known as the negativity effect, describes this mindset – when an experience that affects us adversely (intrusive thoughts, emotions, social interactions, harmful or traumatic events) has a greater impact on our psychological state and processes than neutral or positive experiences of equal intensity.

Research suggests that one reason for this is that not all emotions are of equal value to us. Negative stimuli are thought to have 'greater informational value than positive', which requires 'greater attention and cognitive processing'. In other words, negative stimuli stick because our brain perceives them to have more weight and value. Research also suggests that this value comes from adaptive functions critical to our evolution as human beings. So a hugely simplified way to look at why negative criticism affects us so deeply is to consider that our brain is interpreting it as information we need to process in order to evaluate any potential threat to our survival. (I'll try to remember this next time someone is shitty to me on social media – that it's my brain responding to a threat to my evolution.) This also sheds light on why positive stimuli don't carry the same urgency or weight for our brains – they're not connected to threat or danger (although arguably they're very good for our mental health and physical wellbeing).

Take all this information and apply it to receiving negative criticism of our creativity: it's a wonder that any of us ever find the gall to make anything, to take any expression from our souls and turn it into something tangible in the outside world. To make something from nothing. But we do, we do somehow find the gall. As much as negative bias is in us, and is part of us, so is the impulse to create beauty, to express ourselves through our imaginations, and to share our creativity beyond our mind, where it waits, unmade, unborn.

We are hardwired to pay attention to negative stimuli. We're also driven by awe, beauty, wonder and bewilderment. All of it is what makes us human.

In 2015, three years before *The Lost Flowers of Alice Hart* was published, I entered the first three chapters into a competition run by one of Australia's big publishing houses. The prize was a book deal.

I worked on those first three chapters in my Manchester office until my vision was blurred, revising and polishing my writing to the absolute extent of my abilities. With knots of hope in my heart, I entered the competition.

I waited. And waited.

When the rejection email landed in my inbox, it told me little more than that my chapters hadn't made it past the submission stage in the competition. The criticism wasn't explicit. It was just implied: *You are not good enough, your writing is not good enough, this story is not good enough.*

I perceived this response to be negative criticism. The crushing sense of shame I felt for submitting my work was immediate. My mind was a swarm of fearful thoughts: *This is proof that I can't write a novel. This is confirmation that everything I fear about myself and my writing is true — I'm no good. This is the reality check I've been terrified of getting: everything I believe about the worth of Alice Hart and her story, and the way writing it makes me feel, is just a lie I'm telling myself.* The temptation to give up was sucking at my limbs like swamp mud.

But somehow, after receiving that rejection, I fought hard enough inside myself to keep both nostrils above the mud. I thought about how it felt that day Alice arrived at my desk, when I wrote that first line of her life on paper. It was as if she'd looked at me and said, 'Well, it's just the two of us here, and what are you going to do about it?' I remember thinking, *I haven't come this far to only come this far. I'm not giving up on myself. I'm not giving up on Alice.* Giving up was too easy. I knew how not writing felt. It was a pain far worse than receiving the rejection email.

So I gave myself space to feel crushed. I'd learned enough to know that if I denied uncomfortable emotions – fear, sadness, shame, vulnerability, humiliation, rejection – they would only grow and become more difficult to process the next time I felt them. (In my experience, the emotions we push away always come back with greater intensity.) Once I'd given myself that time, I just kept kicking: fighting against post-traumatic stress patterns in my brain, fighting against apathy and giving up on myself or Alice. It meant something to me. Alice needed me in order to exist on paper, and I wasn't going to abandon her. I wasn't going to abandon myself. I felt a fire deep in my heart, and I knew that I wouldn't let it go out. I decided that implied negative criticism wasn't going to stop me from continuing to write Alice's story.

Practise accompanying yourself instead of abandoning yourself.

A year later, I signed with a literary agency. At the end of 2016, my agents submitted *The Lost Flowers of Alice Hart* to publishers. They sent out exactly the same chapters I'd entered into the competition in 2015, along with the rest of the manuscript.

The publishing company that had run the competition and rejected my chapters was one of the companies that made a bid to publish it.

This experience taught me an invaluable lesson: what if I'd taken that one instance of implied negative outer criticism as Truth? What if I'd never finished writing *The Lost Flowers of Alice Hart*? I cannot begin to imagine what would have become of me if I'd accepted that Truth and stopped writing – honestly, like that photo of Artax in the swamp, it hurts too much to contemplate.

Tacked up near my writing desk is a quote from Theodore Roosevelt that I first came across while reading Brene Brown's book *Daring Greatly* about a decade ago. Roosevelt originally wrote it in 1910 and used male pronouns. I have taken the liberty of tweaking it; if the quote resonates with you, I suggest you do the same.

It is not the critic who counts; not the woman who points out how the strong woman stumbles or where the doer of deeds could have done them better. The credit belongs to the woman who is actually in the arena, whose face is marred by dust and sweat and blood; who strives valiantly; who errs, who comes short again and again, because there is no effort without error and shortcoming; but who does actually strive to do the deeds; who knows the great enthusiasms, the great devotions; who spends herself in a worthy cause; who at the best knows in the end the triumph of high achievement, and who at the worst, if she fails, at least fails while daring greatly, so that her place shall never be with those cold and timid souls who neither know victory nor defeat.

When we create, we are in the arena. Daring greatly. Full of great enthusiasms, full of great devotions. We have skin in the game.

When anyone criticises us for creating, for bleeding our hearts on paper, so to speak, if they're not in the arena, not striving to put their hearts on the line, then they're likely 'cold and timid souls who neither know victory nor defeat'. What value could their response to our work have for us if they've never dared to follow their enthusiasms and devotions? This doesn't mean that being on the receiving end of their criticism about our creativity doesn't hurt like fucking hell. It does mean, though, that we can choose what value we give it. If your critic isn't in the arena, they probably don't have skin in the game. They probably don't know 'the triumph of high achievement', or the poignant grace of 'failing while daring greatly'. They might only be able to wish that they know what you do. That's why they don't get to be your critic, no matter what they say. They don't get to tell you who you are as an artist.

Holly, seven years old, at her own first writing desk

On the Instagram account for his Mojo Mindset Course, Ben Crowe talks about the power of what he calls 'generous assumptions' and shares words he attributes to Walt Whitman: 'Be curious, not judgemental.' Crowe identifies negative media as the cause of the opinions and judgements we tend to adopt about everything, rather than making our own objective assessment and accepting that 'nothing is ever that good or bad, it just is what it is'. Crowe says that with this assessment and acceptance we can block out the noise and be less judgemental, more curious.

He recommends being consciously generous in our assumptions, every day, and suggests that when someone upsets us, we ask ourselves, 'What is the most generous assumption I can make as to why that person did that? And then watch empathy and compassion fill the space.'

Like all of us, I've been on the receiving end of criticism throughout my life, both personal and, since I became an author in 2018, public. One of the things I find hardest to remember about people harshly criticising me or my work is that their criticism is coming from *them*. From who they are, as they are, and how they are perceiving and relating to me and my work. When they put their criticism on the internet, for example, and I see it, it feels like a harpoon through my heart. But when I use the generous assumption tactic that Ben Crowe talks about, it allows me to put some distance between myself and whatever they say about me, or my writing, or my work as co-host on the TV documentary series *Back to Nature*, or anything that I've created and shared from my heart. And then I can see that it's actually not about me. It's about the critic. Who they are. It's not information that tells me who I am. It doesn't get to stop me from creating. I listen to myself to know who I am. I write because I know how it makes me feel and know it's how I give myself joy and offer my art in service of others.

Alok Vaid-Menon, internationally renowned gender non-conforming writer and performance artist, has discussed how they manage to love people who hate them. The answer, they say, is to 'remember they were once a baby too ... and then something hurt them so much they began to correlate new experiences with fear'.

The value of making generous assumptions about our outer critics is that the empathy and compassion it creates works both ways. It is an extension of grace and humanity to our critics. In turn, it's an offering of grace and humanity to ourselves. A way to ease our own suffering and allow us to get back to listening to ourselves, to know who we are, and to hear the call of our inner country.

In the spirit of playfulness, I'll add that it can be very powerful, if you've absorbed painful outer criticism, to give yourself the chance to release it in a way that doesn't harm you or anyone else. I highly recommend playing Lily Allen's 'Fuck You' at ear-splitting volume. And, of course, dancing and singing along louder than your sound system.

Truth: if I try to write to be liked by everyone, to avoid criticism, to keep everyone happy, I won't write anything meaningful. Writing that wants to be likeable isn't writing that comes from the tender and true place inside me. It's writing that comes from the people-pleasing place inside me, diluted, agreeable and without conviction. I take a cue from Eleanor Roosevelt, who said, 'Do what you feel in your heart to be right – for you'll be criticized anyway. You'll be damned if you do, and damned if you don't.'

Truth: emotions and our ability to feel them are not weaknesses. Emotions make us human. Add imagination, and emotions make us capable of working magic. In 2017, on a mindfulness and self-compassion retreat in the Netherlands with clinical psychologist Chris Germer and academic Kristin Neff, whose advice on self-compassion I quoted earlier, I sat in a room of one hundred people. Germer asked us, 'What's the meaning of being human? What's our purpose?' We sat together, quietly. He smiled, and after a while said simply, 'To feel.' Recalling that now in the context of art and creativity, I'm reminded of Jack Kerouac's words, 'Goddam it, FEELING is what I like in art, not CRAFTINESS and the hiding of feelings.'

A pact: let's create what we feel is right in our hearts. And be damned together.

Something to think about: every single piece of art you've ever loved so much it feels like you'll stop breathing has been equally intensely hated by someone else. Cate Blanchett has haters, Beyoncé has haters (I shudder to even type that). In 2002 I was in Seattle, Pearl Jam's hometown, walking back from where they'd just played a sold-out show that had moved me to tears and, on the giddy walk back to our hostel, my friends and I passed a diner. Inside, a group of people sat by the window holding up napkins on which they'd written *PEARL JAM SUCKS*. Each of them was also flipping us, the crowds pouring from Key Arena, the middle finger. I've never forgotten it. As much as I loved Pearl Jam's music, particularly Eddie Vedder's voice, which had soothed and guided me through intense years of my life, it was equally hated by others. I was bewildered by the revelation: not even my beloved Pearl Jam were immune from criticism.

Please enjoy the following one-star reviews of some of the best-loved art in our lives:

1. So far, I have found that this book is complete drivel. I don't understand the mass appeal to this novel, nor do I understand how it managed to go down in history as an amazing piece of American literature. This book has no plot, no point, and no real characters.

2. This was one of the worst books I have ever read. I am still upset [that] I wasted the time reading about 2 miserable people who instead of just being miserable together, ruin a bunch of other people's lives in the process.

3. [They] are not merely awful; I would consider it sacrilegious to say anything less than that they are god awful. They are so

unbelievably horrible, so appallingly unmusical, so dogmatically insensitive to the magic of the art …

4. I feel dirty for watching this. If you like this movie, you are a fucking idiot.

5. A bit repetitious about muddy puddles.

6. This movie is for psychopaths and psychopaths only. It is portraying stalking as a symbol of love and affection and quite frankly that should not be okay. I'm not sure if they ban movies, but this one deserves to be banned. It is promoting a horrible message. People cannot think this is okay. I am horrified.

7. It's a heart-warming story, but it's just not believable.

And here are the works and artists they refer to:

1. *To Kill a Mockingbird*
2. *Wuthering Heights*
3. The Beatles
4. *Dirty Dancing*
5. *The Story of Peppa Pig*
6. *Sleepless in Seattle*
7. *E.T.*

Towards the end of my second novel, *The Seven Skins of Esther Wilding*, Esther is at a harbour in the Faroe Islands when she sees an orange starfish under the sea, clinging to one of the jetty pontoons. The sight reminds her of her father, Jack, an avid nature-lover. Esther remembers being a kid at the sea with Jack in Lutruwita/Tasmania when he told her that in the North Atlantic, starfish can regenerate their own arms if they lose them and, even more incredibly, if the severed arm is not harmed, it can regenerate a whole body and create a genetically identical starfish.

Outer criticism, even the fear of receiving outer criticism, might feel like it's going to hurt so much that it will somehow sever parts of us from ourselves. But, as Frida Kahlo said, 'At the end of the day, we can endure much more than we think we can.'

We can be starfish. Able to regenerate, even after threat. Able to grow. Able to go on creating and be whole.

Every time my creativity suffers a knock from outer criticism – not only my writing has been criticised, but also my body, mind, self-expression, face and voice – I return over and over again to the only person who can tell me who I am. She's about fourteen years old and she's typing away on a refurbished IBM computer like her life depends on it. I think about what I'm creating in my writing and what I want to create with my writing, and I check in with that kid. That's who I listen to. That's who I honour when I wear flowers and butterflies in my hair. I'm the adult I am because she's the kid she was. As Ursula K. Le Guin wrote, 'I believe that maturity is not an outgrowing, but a growing up: that an adult is not a dead child, but a child who survived.' That fourteen-year-old is who matters to me, more than what anyone not in the arena alongside me has to say.

I promise you: if I can weather such harsh outer criticism and keep creating, keep writing, you can too.

If I'm too much in my own head when I'm writing and feel myself tangled up in fears of what other people are going to think of what I'm creating, I practise asking myself one question: *Do I love what I'm writing?*

An adage about writing is 'Write what you know'. If I might offer an additional way of thinking about facing the blank page of your creativity: make what you love. What causes your heart to ache. What you dream of, imagine, yearn for, wish was different, rage against, can't live without …

Before I'd finished writing *The Lost Flowers of Alice Hart*, before I had an agent or was published, I was confused, thinking that becoming a novelist meant I should be focused on the outer writing landscape as much as the interior – agents, publishers, networking, social media, writing tips. Focusing on those exterior elements has its place, but it didn't get my first novel written. The only thing that did was protecting the magic of my inner country – my imagination – and my self-discipline. I realised I had to choose to use my will, over and over again, to show up and to write every day, for however long I could. And writing was not always clacking away at my keyboard. It was staring at café walls and out of bus windows and into my garden and thinking about Alice Hart's story. Thinking about moving it along. Every time I returned to my manuscript to write another line, I developed a habit of focusing on that one question: *Do I love what I'm writing?*

It felt to me that creating the world of a novel alone and writing it alone was hard enough. So while I was writing, whenever fear made me falter or stumble (which was every day), that question became my touchstone: *Do I love what I'm writing?*

If my answer was ambivalent, I knew I needed more staring-into-space time to think, daydream and recentre myself in the story until I felt reconnected. Until I felt that love firing in my belly once more. I came back to this question again throughout the process of writing *The Seven Skins of Esther Wilding*: *Do I love what I'm writing?*

I want to end this chapter with another question.

Whose house?

Your house.

This is your house, on your inner country. Built of the joy your creativity brings you. Your hopefulness, your courage, your imagination, the fire in your heart. You get to say who you let in. You get to say what power they have while they're there.

Whose house? Your house.

As I've mentioned, one of the biggest threats outer criticism can pose to our creativity – if we haven't developed the Mirren muscles to respond to it in a preserving way – is that the fear of it will stop us from creating.

One of the ways this can manifest is through overthinking and resistance, which, combined, can cause us to reach a stalemate in our creativity – otherwise known as creative block.

OUTER CRITIC + RESILIENCE PROVOCATIONS

When the outer critic comes, will you give up or become a starfish and keep on growing and following your joy?

What if Artax's Swamp of Sadness became Peppa Pig's muddy puddles that we could dance and splash around in without getting sucked down?

Does the thought of creating whatever calls to you to be made change at all when you consider that it's protected by your house, on your inner country?

This is your house of creative joy … Who and what will you let in? And who and what – with compassion – can get the fuck out?

What's one thing you could do right now to honour that spark of creativity inside you?

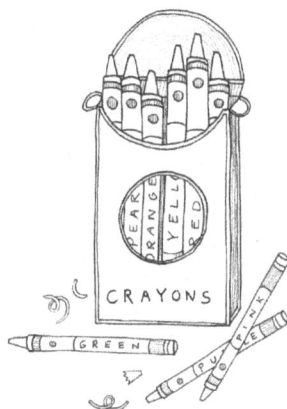

7

Creative Block + Daydream Machine: Sniffing Pink Flamingo

Creative block is the often-overwhelming experience of wanting to create but feeling utterly stuck in the process, without any ability to gain traction. (An image that comes to mind whenever I think about creative block is a vehicle bogged in mud, wheels spinning but with no forward momentum.) It can happen to every artist, in every art form and every type of creative process.

It might feel the same for many of us, but can be completely different for others.

This is what creative block can look like for me: I show up at my desk, ready and raring to write, either by hand or typing. I practise my rituals – jot down some notes of intention for my ideas that I'm going to work from, light a candle with a chosen essential oil, say a prayer of conscious thanks to the land I'm writing on – then I pick up my pen or turn on my laptop … and find myself squirming. Restless. No words come. I fidget. I procrastinate. Faff about flicking through books, scrolling through distractions in my emails or social media. Go back to my page or Word document. Nothing. The river's run dry.

In my body, creative block feels like there's something stuck in my throat. It's lodged in my windpipe or my chest. Sometimes it feels as though I can't take full, deep breaths. My head pounds. At its worst, this sensation of feeling stuck has caused me such anxiety that I've ended up retching. Even when it's not that severe, I find the stasis of creative block painful, frustrating and distressing.

Sometimes it takes conscious awareness and time with Bullshit-o-Meter to figure out if I'm procrastinating or if I'm in creative block, because, like self-doubt and the inner critic, the two can feel like bedfellows to me. Again, it might be different for you. For me there's a clear difference in how I experience them. Procrastination is when I have the story and ideas but I avoid writing them (for countless reasons). Creative block is when the story and ideas aren't there, yet I keep trying to write like they are.

Before I learned how to work with creative block, I would stay at my desk, stewing in discomfort, telling myself I just needed to stick at it, wait it out. The words would come. But the longer I stayed at my desk, the more it felt like I was scraping around aimlessly inside my empty, dusty mind, looking for water. Instead of stepping away and trying a new way to engage my imagination, I persisted, thinking that if I left my desk I was giving up or quitting. So I did the same thing again and again. Stayed at my desk but expected a different outcome. Every time, I came up empty-handed. Every time I stayed in that state, I sank deeper and deeper into a kind of creative paralysis, with no story, no ideas, no beautiful sentences, no vivid scenes. Nothing but imagined dust under my fingernails, a parched mind and a crushed spirit to show for my efforts. That's when all the forces I work hard to keep at bay would most often swoop in. Past trauma-informed narratives, fear, failure, self-doubt, perfectionism, procrastination, my inner critic, my outer critics – they would all gather in my mind for a raucous, free-for-all party, passing around nibblies and raising a toast to their success, having quashed my creative thinking for the day.

Sound familiar?

When it happens to me now, I recognise it as a sign. Telling me that being at my desk is not what I need for my writing or my creativity. Telling me to get up, walk away and spend some time intentionally seeking wonder, possibility, joy. In other words, to crank up my daydream machine.

Over the past fifteen years I've been writing, I've tried, tried, tried again, and learned, slowly, how to build my daydream machine. It's not, of course, a literal machine. It's an imagined one, a knockabout, magical, mysterious contraption, kind of akin to Bullshit-o-Meter, that I can use anytime I need to bring to life a world I want to write about. (If you've seen the Gene Wilder film adaptation *Willy Wonka and the Chocolate Factory*, you'll know the kind of contraption I imagine, something like the Great Gum Machine.) Basically, my daydream machine is something I imagine feeding my ideas into, even if they're just half-formed. It brings these ideas to life so vividly that they feel real to me.

What's actually happening is that I'm making and taking time to think deeply about my ideas, holding them lightly and loosely as I brainstorm, letting myself consider possibilities, beyond the harsh and judgemental gaze of my inner critic. When I think deeply like this, when I'm in this deep state of brainstorming – cranking up the daydream machine – I don't reject any thoughts or ideas. There's no such thing as a bad idea. Every thought is welcome. I grasp ideas that resonate, and release ones that don't. Once an idea feels known to me and I return to my keyboard to write it out, creative block cannot touch it.

I'll give you an example. In *The Lost Flowers of Alice Hart*, after Alice leaves the coastal sugar cane landscapes of her childhood home – which I knew myself from places where I grew up – she goes with her grandmother, June, whom she's never met, to June's home, a native Australian flower farm called Thornfield.

Once I got that idea, that Alice would move away from where she grew up to go to live at Thornfield, I went to my desk to write about this place I hadn't yet imagined, sensed or daydreamed to life. At my keyboard I experienced such extreme resistance and discomfort, such an intense choking sensation, that I would have preferred pretty much anything to sitting there, empty-minded, trying to create. Pap smear at 8 am on a Monday instead of writing Alice going to Thornfield? Sign me up. In that state of resistance, avoidance and discomfort, my anxiety around writing, my self-doubt, inner critic and sense of perfectionism all intensified. At one point, I was so convinced that Thornfield was a terrible idea – I couldn't 'see' it, I didn't 'know' it – that I came close to scrapping it altogether and giving up on the entire novel.

Then I put it through my daydream machine: I walked away from my desk, and instead started collecting images and pieces of writing about flower farming from books, magazines and the internet. I went for long walks. I let my imagination go, I allowed *and* encouraged myself to dream Thornfield to life. I gave myself time to gather ideas, to go inwards, to dwell in my inner country. Slowly, organically and naturally, June, the Flowers (the women who run the farm), and the fields and walls at Thornfield took shape, person by person, bulb by bulb and room by room. Eventually, Thornfield became so real to me that at one point I felt pained I couldn't get in my car and drive there myself.

This experience helped me understand how vital daydreaming is to creativity, and to managing creative block. To managing feeling stuck. Daydreaming is how I feed my mind and prepare myself to create. The act of doing it with purpose, meaning and intention lets my mind know that I'm getting ready to write. Daydreaming also soothes me, and prevents me from feeling overwhelmed by the task at hand, the act of creating. If I don't daydream before I go to my desk and I turn up without knowing what I'm writing, if I don't have images or feelings or themes that I've already dreamed to life in my mind before I go to my keyboard, I get taken out by anxiety and can't write. I suffer the choking feeling again. Creative block overwhelms me. All the pleasure and joy are gone. To quote Gore Vidal, 'The unfed mind devours itself.'

I'd bet my favourite mint-green fountain pen that if you're reading this book, the odds are probably high that someone has told you at some point in your life to 'Get your head out of the clouds and stop daydreaming.' As doctor and science writer Alison Escalante writes, 'Daydreaming has been under attack for generations.' But a recent study into daydreaming suggests it's an important skill that has benefits for our mental health and wellbeing. The study showed that, in basic terms, adults are pretty shit at daydreaming. 'This is part of our cognitive toolkit that's underdeveloped, and it's kind of sad,' writes psychology professor and author of the study, Erin Westgate. She argues that while the good news is that daydreaming is something we can get better at doing, the not-so-good news is that we don't 'intuitively understand how to think enjoyable thoughts ... We don't seem to know what to think about to have a positive experience.' Results from her study with participants who were prompted to think 'meaningful thoughts' were surprising: Westgate expected that they'd have a pleasant experience, but it was the opposite – participants found the task of intentionally thinking about something meaningful to be more unpleasant than free thinking. After learning from participants what they'd thought about during the exercise, Westgate said, 'It was heavy stuff. It didn't seem to occur to [participants] that they could use the time to enjoy their own thoughts.'

Westgate's work suggests that when we're prompted to daydream, we might err towards superficial pleasures like eating a perfect slice of cake – but sadly, those thoughts don't have the same beneficial effect as those that are 'pleasant but also meaningful'. After Westgate shared a list of pleasant and meaningful example thoughts with the participants, they reportedly 'enjoyed thinking 50% more than when they were instructed to think about whatever they wanted'. This is thinking that, Westgate says, 'you can harness in your everyday life by prompting yourself with topics you'd find rewarding to daydream about, like a pleasant memory, future accomplishment, or an event you're looking forward to'.

While daydreaming is an important life skill, it is also, to me, an essential skill in my Toolkit of Unfuckable-with Magic. To understand how vital daydreaming is to my writing, I have had to learn to give myself permission to assert the value of my inner country. And to acknowledge that accessing it requires me to spend purposeful and meaningful time daydreaming about it. I won't mince words: it's been one of the hardest fucking things I've ever learned in my writing. Because, as I'm sure you do too, I have ingrained in me a lifetime of hearing daydreaming being criticised as 'childish'. I was both alarmed and reassured to know I'm not alone; another study, conducted by the University of Florida, found that '67% of men and 25% of women preferred to give themselves an electric shock than be alone with their thoughts'.

Erin Westgate assures us that daydreaming is nothing to be ashamed of, and is something instead to cultivate, because it 'sets us apart. It defines our humanity. It allows us to imagine new realities. But that kind of thinking requires practice.' Part of practising daydreaming is about trusting that 'it's possible to have a good experience if you prime your brain with topics that you'll find pleasant', Westgate says. 'This is something all of us can do once you have the concept. We give four- and five-year-olds these instructions, and it makes sense to them.'

Westgate comforts us with the reminder that daydreaming is 'hard for everybody. There's no good evidence that some types of people are simply better thinkers. I'm the world's worst person at this: I would definitely rather have the electric shock. But knowing why it can be hard and what makes it easier really makes a difference. The encouraging part is we can all get better.'

Another benefit of building and developing our daydreaming skills, Westgate says, is the 'source of enjoyable thoughts' we create, which we can access during times of stress. 'What we feel is a function of what we think. Thinking for pleasure can be a powerful tool to shape our emotions.' If you've ever loved creating, making stuff, writing, dancing, singing, gardening or being away with the fairies, like me, you'll know this to be inherently true: when we're daydreaming or thinking for pleasure, it affects our mindset and emotional state. On an otherwise dull day, if I've spent time thinking deeply about the world of a novel in my mind, I experience a sense of meaning, awe, purpose, wonder and joy, which increases the quality of my day and my state of mind. Westgate's study is an encouraging examination of daydreaming, and we can all draw on its findings to enhance our creative lives.

When I was writing *The Seven Skins of Esther Wilding* during Covid lockdowns, there were countless mornings when I woke up feeling like I was almost choking on anxiety-induced creative block. Feeling helpless, I started going out for purposeful daydreaming walks with Sam, so that I could move and breathe and talk out the tangles in my mind. As we fell into rhythm beside each other, my thinking seemed to follow. My mind would settle and ideas would start to form, gather, connect and rain down on me. I'd set out stressed and come home euphoric. In creativity terms, it was my Drew-Barrymore-in-the-rain moment. (Google 'drew barrymore rain' if you haven't seen the video.) Sometimes I only needed a thirty-minute walk to go from tangles to daydream rain. Sometimes, it took ninety minutes. But walking with the purpose of talking out all the thickets and brambles inside me until I could connect with a place of thinking for pleasure in my mind is one of the most powerful tools I've found and experienced for activating daydreaming in my creativity.

There's another kind of daydreaming that I find fascinating and deeply love when it happens to me. It's the daydreaming we experience without even having to try.

According to mental health and mindfulness organisation Headspace, psychologists have suggested that 'the ability to combine existing ideas or information in new ways is more important for creativity than trying to produce ideas out of thin air'. They say that 'our brains are constantly forming new connections between regions that process memories, knowledge and challenges, without us even being aware of it'. During this subconscious processing, 'our brains bring together information in a meaningful way that results in a new idea, or a "eureka moment," which appears to come out of nowhere'.

This rings true for me: I have been moaning for years that I need a waterproof notebook to hang in the shower for all the ideas I get while I'm in there. As Headspace explains, 'Fascinatingly, these types of lightbulb moments seem more likely to happen when we're doing something passive like taking a shower, driving to work or trying to fall asleep, rather than when we're explicitly trying to be creative.'

I learned this to be true when I was working on my first draft of *The Lost Flowers of Alice Hart*. Writing was not just the act of typing on my keyboard; it was also was sitting on the bus and daydreaming. It was sitting in cafés and people-watching. It was hiking on the moors, it was swimming in the Irish Sea, it was chopping veggies for dinner, and doing washing and vacuuming.

My writing, my creativity, happened in so many more places, spaces and moments than just those I spent at my desk. It was the processing happening in my brain on days I stayed away from my desk completely. It was the deep thinking I did while I was intentionally looking at other people's art, potting plants, and strolling between weekend market stalls. Creativity, I found, breeds creativity. Being around other people's creations, and observing creativity in nature – the bud of a new leaf, bees gathering pollen, flowers in bloom – fuelled my own.

While writing this chapter, I call my friend Zoe Rimmer. We've made a date to talk about creativity, creative blocks, how they feel, and how we manage them. Zoe is a Pakana woman from Lutruwita/Tasmania who is an artist, currently studying for a PhD, and has an extensive background in gallery curation.

I start our conversation with a super-easy, not-at-all-complex question. 'What is creativity?' We both laugh at the absurdity of it. 'Let me rephrase, Zo. Tell me what creativity is to *you*?'

Zoe shares that much of her creative thinking has always been spread across the diverse aspects of her work, which have included writing; academia; curation; working with cultural, historic, museum-type collections and exhibitions; and working with artists. For the past twelve months, she's been working full time on her PhD, and at the point when we speak, Zoe shares with me that she's feeling uncreative. I ask why.

'Because I'm mostly alone in a sterile office, working by myself, trying to meld my creativity into what is basically just a big, rigid academic document, full of references.'

I groan in empathy.

'I feel a little bit like creativity gets beaten out of the academic and education system in general,' Zoe muses. 'It's all about following a formula, so that, in a way, everything sort of becomes the same in the process, and individual creativity evaporates.'

We talk about how difficult it is to nurture creativity when you're feeling particularly boxed in or blocked, and why it's important to do that. Zoe tells me about a recent experience when she felt stuck, under time pressure to write the concluding chapter of her PhD. At the same time an opportunity came up: she was invited to go on Country, rafting down the Franklin River. Her impulse was clear: she wanted to go. But she declined. Told herself she had to stay focused and write her chapter. A few days later though, she realised how much she'd regret not going on the trip, left her chapter, and went and spent ten days on the river and on Country.

'I was so present during those ten days, focused on rafting the river, setting up camp, cooking, trying to stay warm, trying to keep the leeches off me, and in amongst all of that, having profound moments of just being on Country. Feeling connected. When I got home, back to my work, my concluding chapter just flowed out of me. My whole trip on River Country – learning about the rediscovery of Kuti Kina Cave and the campaign to save the Franklin River and that whole cultural landscape from being dammed – it all became part of my conclusion. For our community, reconnecting with Country and reconnecting with culture revives our creative, artistic and spiritual practices. I'd been writing about it for months in my PhD but forgot somewhere along the way that I need to actually do it.'

Zoe and I talk a little bit about kanalaritja, the ancient cultural practice of shell gathering, cleaning and stringing by Pakana women that 'extends far beyond living memory'. Kanalaritja is living creativity, unbroken through time – Pakana women have continued this cultural expression and practice through invasion, war and colonisation.

'My trip on the river reminded me that even if it's just a day out on the beach collecting shells, that's what my creativity needs, that's what helps me,' Zoe says, 'to revive and reconnect with Country and culture. My connection to Country and my connection to my creativity always need tending. Sometimes I get a bit anxious and think, "I don't have time to be doing this, I've got so much work to do," but actually going on Country and restoring my creativity and spirit never hinders but always helps my work.'

I ask Zoe how she manages creative block in her day-to-day life. One of her go-to tools is changing the environment she's working in. Often, she'll leave the office to take her laptop to a cosy café or library.

'What about when you feel that creative itch in your fingertips, an urge to make something, outside of your work?' I ask.

'If I want to intentionally make something, then it usually involves getting my aunty or my mum or my daughter together and we go on a road trip. Head to one of our places. Again, it's connecting with Country. It's also being with my family, sharing in our purpose, culture and creativity. Sometimes we'll just be driving, and my aunty will see river reeds, and we have to pull over and grab some. We never know what we're going to make. Whatever we gather – plants, shells – they tell us what we're going to create. I really like working with kelp and grasses, weaving and basket-making. I don't ever worry about how whatever I'm making is going to turn out. It's intuitive. Eventually it'll be something. And even if it's really wonky, it's what it's meant to be and I love it. I feel like the materials we work with – reeds, grasses, kelp, shells – they have their own story that you have to follow. Trying to control what I create because I want it to become something absolutely perfect is when it doesn't work for me.'

I ask Zoe how she experiences perfectionism and all its manifestations, like self-doubt, her inner critic, fear.

She nods, knowingly. 'It's such a trap. In the context of my PhD, the pressure of having original ideas and thinking is a big blocker for me.'

'How do you stop yourself becoming entrapped by it, by perfectionism?'

'I go back to my community,' Zoe answers. 'Our creativity is a collective thing. We all make baskets or kanalaritja, but they're all so different. When you come together as a collective and share ideas and conversations, that's when, for me, creativity starts to spark again. By contrast, academia is so focused on the individual and it's very competitive. I don't like to work like that.'

Before we end our chat, Zoe shares with me why creativity is deeply important and powerful to her: because, historically in Australia, the creativity of First Nations people has been oppressed and dictated by non-Aboriginal people, and this continues today.

'Going onto Country with my aunty, mum and daughter, to follow our creative instinct and practise our culture, doesn't just give us joy. It brings us connection. It builds our resilience. Creativity is how we express ourselves individually and communally. And it's about resistance. Our creativity is an act of resistance, to create whatever we are called to create, particularly here, in Lutruwita/Tasmania, where we were told for such a long time that Aboriginal people didn't exist. Our freedom of expression through creativity is one of the ways we resist.'

Listening to Zoe's approach and instincts around creativity – something she does as a collective, with community – was deeply moving, and reminded me of something very valuable about creativity in general. Which is that, particularly when addressing creative block, sometimes we need to be with others. My own sense of community comes from untangling my daydreaming on walks with Sam and sharing my ideas with a few trusted people who are also writers and artists (they're in the arena, they have skin in the game). Other writers might thrive by joining a writing group for support, encouragement and help to work through problems or blockages. With different art forms, maybe it's doing a class, joining an online forum or volunteering at an arts centre, and sharing creativity in these communities.

Talking with Zoe also reminded me how integral improvisation and spontaneity can be to daydreaming and creativity. In 2008, a group of US-based neuroscientists conducted MRI brain scans of jazz musicians before and while they made improvised music. They concluded that when the musicians were improvising there was a significant decrease of activity in the region of the

Just create *something*. Anything.

brain known as the dorsolateral prefrontal cortex. This region is usually active when we're focused on set tasks, and it can help us ignore distractions. Although that might be great during an exam or interview, this function of our brain – to filter out or inhibit distracting external information – can be detrimental to our creative thinking by limiting our brain's 'ability to form spontaneous ideas and connections'.

It was precisely through improvising – creating freely, simultaneously – that the jazz musicians reduced activity in the prefrontal cortex of the brain and limited the brain's filtering of 'distracting' information. Sometimes the way to overcome creative block is to get out of our own way, out of our own heads, just create *something*. Anything.

Before I started writing this book, I intuitively had the idea in my head that I needed to get comfortable with the discomfort of improvisational creativity. I went to a stationery shop and bought an A3 art journal and a box of Crayola crayons. Once I started to write the prologue and was regularly balking at the page, I knew from experience that I needed to step away. I sat in the breeze coming through my window, opened my art journal, flipped back the cardboard lid on the box and stared at the crayons. At the blank page.

Let's be clear here: I am not a practising visual artist. Until that moment, I didn't think I was into drawing. I had to stop and think about the last time I'd drawn anything. I figured it had been at least twenty years, not since high school, when my friends and I drew love hearts in the margins of each other's exercise books, and butterflies and flowers on each other's skin at lunchtimes.

I sat there in the breeze, staring at the blank page, kind of amused and kind of bewildered by how much it intimidated me. *Just create*, I thought. I walked my fingers through the crayons. Picked one. Took it out of the box. Then lifted it to my nose and sniffed it. *What the fuck are you doing?* I laughed at myself. And yet I sniffed it again. Then I sniffed the whole box of crayons. The waxy smell stirred up long-forgotten memories of how exciting paper and crayons used to be to me when I was young. I never wondered then if I could draw. I just reached for handfuls of crayons and relished the colour, waxy texture, and the lines and strokes as I drew. The joy of drawing deepened when I learned to read and became besotted with the names of each crayon colour. From then on, the colours were major deciding factors in whatever masterpiece I was drawing, based on the images they conjured in my imagination. Banana Mania. Caribbean Green. Sunset Orange. My favourite was Pink Flamingo.

I sat in my chair sniffing crayons and letting myself choose colours and move my crayons over the paper. An hour passed in what felt like minutes. And I remembered: I'd really loved it. I'd loved to draw. Which I wouldn't have rediscovered if I hadn't sat down with the blank page, told myself not to overthink it,

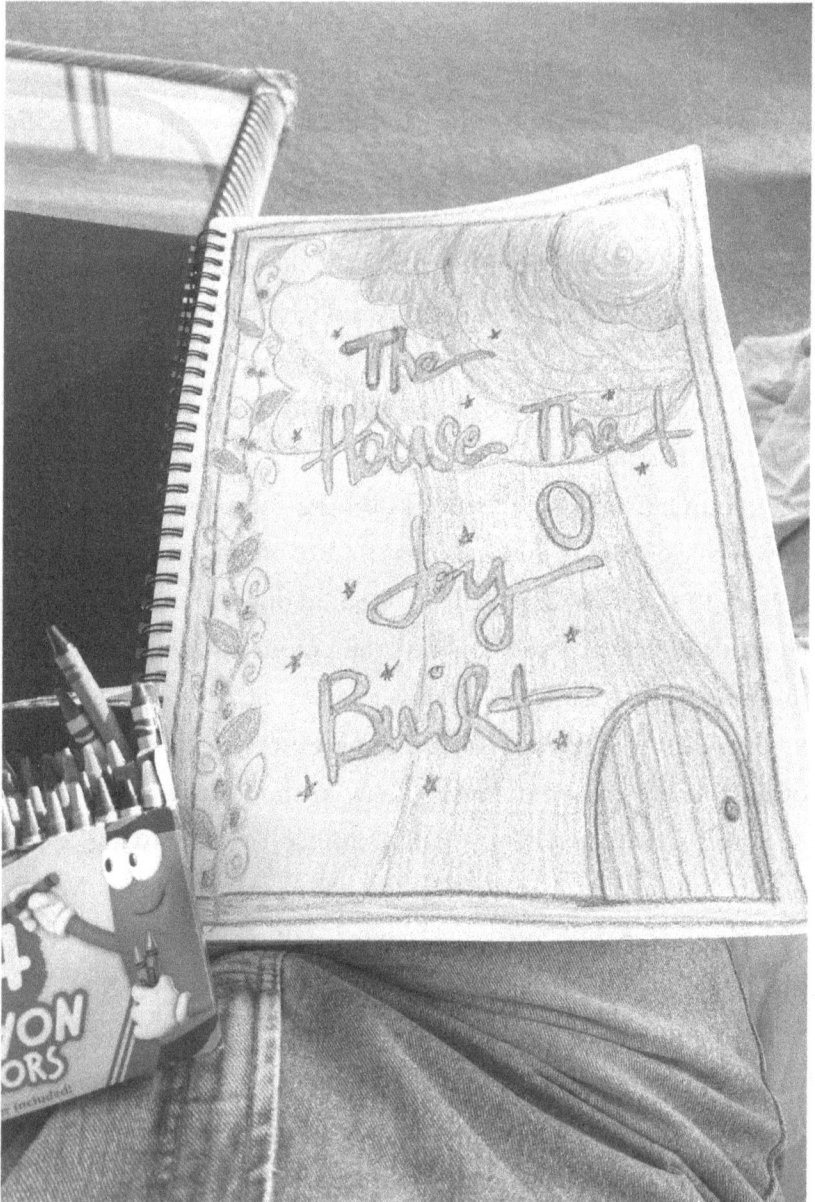

Holly's art journal, 2023

and allowed myself to watch what happened when I put my Pink Flamingo crayon to paper.

What if you feel so overwhelmed by creative block that you don't even know what you love to create, and so can't begin to daydream about it?

What if you don't hear a call from your inner country?

What if the path within is so overgrown that you can't feel or sense one idea blooming?

Give yourself permission to take your time.

Ask yourself what you loved as a kid.

Open a box of crayons and sniff them.

Allow yourself to remember.

And if you can't remember anything you've loved, give yourself permission to be curious. Prioritise your curiosity as a matter of psychological life and death. (This next sentiment calls for a bit of drama. And, actually, caps lock.)

GIVE YOURSELF PERMISSION TO PRIORITISE
FEEDING YOUR HEART AND YOUR MIND.

But how to do that? Feed your heart and mind?

Take yourself into places and spaces that seem interesting to you. Pay attention to how you feel when you're in them and around them. Pay attention to what makes your heart race, your eyes water and your chest swell. To the flutter in your belly and the tingle in your fingers when you are awed. To the loosening of your jaw, and the stillness in your mind when you feel wonder. Our bodies often have the answers we're searching for.

Pay attention and follow these signs. They are the sustaining sweet crumbs that will lead you into the daydream machine in your imagination. Your inner country is always waiting for you.

In her book *This Is Not a Book about Benedict Cumberbatch*, Tabitha Carvan implores us to find what we love, what lights us up inside, what stirs our creativity, inspiration and desire, and let ourselves love it like our lives depend on it. Because, she argues, the quality of our lives *does* depend on it. She asks her reader, 'Do you know what it is that you love? Not who – I already know you love the most important people in your life – but what. And if you didn't have to explain or defend it, would that change anything for you? … Have you made yourself available to love the full suite of things that might move you? Or [have you] been cut off at the pass, diverted toward things that seem more important? If … I told you … that not everything … has to be justifiable as a good use of your time or mind, could you then let [yourself] find [your] way toward loving what [you] love? And what would that look like for you?'

Love what you love, without shame. Crank up your daydream machine and feed your mind, without shame. Value your creativity and inner country, without shame.

It's as simple and as hard as that. Particularly when fear convinces you that when it comes to being an artist, you're nothing but an imposter.

CREATIVE BLOCK + DAYDREAM MACHINE PROVOCATIONS

How much do you value and make space for daydreaming in your life?

Is your daydream machine cranked up and ready to go or rusting in the shed covered in dust?

What would you think about if you were thinking for pleasure?

What spaces, places and activities cause sparks in your heart, mind and imagination?

What is one thing your house on your inner country would definitely have?

The collective noun for a gathering of pink flamingos is a flamboyance. How perfect is that? How flamboyant might you make your daydream machine and what kind of community might gather around the joy that you're daydreaming about?

8

Imposter Syndrome + You Belong Here: There's No Place Like It

If a book could serenade its reader, when you reach this final chapter, I would love for the opening bars of Vanessa Williams's 'Save the Best for Last' to begin right about … now. I can't think of a better song to accompany our exploration of imposter syndrome.

As you might know first-hand, imposter syndrome is something we can all experience. It's comprised of everything (and more) that's led us to this page: fear, self-doubt, failure, procrastination, inner critic, outer critic and creative block. At the heart of imposter syndrome is the belief that we are not enough. Not good enough. Smart enough. Worthy enough. Expert enough. Skilled enough. Just not enough. The belief that anything we have achieved, or anything that results from our hard work, has nothing to do with us. That it was simply luck, chance, fate, a roll of the dice.

If we are guided by the belief that we are imposters and frauds, and our achievements do not belong to us – that we do not *belong* – then there are untold rooms of our lives we don't enter. When we think we don't belong somewhere, we miss chance after chance to stake a claim on our experience, our imagination, our creativity. We don't take a seat at the table. We miss out.

In 2014, following the death in my family, I felt displaced by shock and grief. Like I belonged nowhere. Sometimes I took comfort in reading about grieving, and I became particularly fond of two quotes. One was from Shakespeare's *King Lear*: 'Nothing can come of nothing, speak again.' The other, an Alcoholics Anonymous mantra: 'Nothing changes if nothing changes.'

Both quotes stuck to me like burrs in that time when I felt outside myself, as I tried to come to terms with death, loss, grief, life, joy and living. It was as if I was suspended in a state of nothingness. Wanting to understand the way I was feeling, I sought out a copy of *The Neverending Story*. There was a conversation that I vaguely remembered from the book, and I was desperate to re-read it. When I found the excerpt, I was moved by how deeply it resonated with me.

'Is it very painful?' Atreyu asked.

'No,' said the second bark troll, the one with the hole in his chest. 'You don't feel a thing. There's just something missing. And once it gets hold of you, something more is missing every day. Soon there won't be anything left of us.'

The temptation to sever myself from grief, to try and not feel it, was strong. But I found the will to turn away from that allure. I knew the kind of nothing that would come from that nothingness. That would be like living with a hole in my chest. And that, to me, would be wasting my life. I didn't want to go back to that state again.

I became the opposite of numb: ravenous for some kind of comfort. Although I was grieving and my inner country felt far away and inaccessible, I intuitively turned to imagination. Creativity felt like a life-giving force, and in my hunger to fill myself with it, I reached once more for Austin Kleon's books on being an artist, and Julia Cameron's *The Artists' Way*.

Reading the latter for the first time, I was thunderstruck by the blurb on the inside pages. '*The Artist's Way* provides a twelve-week course to guide you through the process of recovering your creative self.' A prickle of goosebumps rushed over my body. I turned to the Contents page. There was that word again: *Recovering*. The twelve main chapters were divided into the twelve weeks of the course, and each chapter title started with the word 'recovering'. 'Week 1: Recovering a Sense of Safety', 'Week 5: Recovering a Sense of Possibility', 'Week 12: Recovering a Sense of Faith'.

I hadn't even made it to the proper first page, but was so overwhelmed by my sense of recognition reading the blurb and contents pages that I had to put the book aside and go out for a walk. It was the first time I understood in a way that actually felt believable to me, that my writing self, which I'd known since I was three years old, wasn't gone from me forever. I realised that the blockage I was suffering – all the ways I feared I wasn't enough and didn't belong – was about maybe more than writing. And to unblock my mind, I needed to go into creative recovery.

So, feeling levelled by bereavement and with nothing to lose, I decided to commit to this twelve-week recovery program. Of my creativity. Of the parts of myself I'd hidden away for too long. Starting with, among other tasks, taking myself on 'artist dates', for the purpose and intention of treating and considering myself as an artist. I was excited, and immediately daunted.

The term 'imposter syndrome' was introduced by the research of Suzanne Imes and Pauline Clance, who published an article in 1978 entitled 'The impostor phenomenon in high achieving women: dynamics and therapeutic intervention'. Since then, further research has shown that anyone can experience imposter syndrome, with the severity and complexity of it depending on a vast range of personal and societal factors such as our privileges, cultural backgrounds and identities.

Imposter syndrome thrives on the feeling that we are not responsible for our self-actualisation, success, accomplishments or achievements. Even people who have been very successful in their chosen fields can feel that their achievements are due more to luck than their own skills or qualities, and they may fear that they can't maintain their success and will eventually be 'found out'.

In my experience, imposter syndrome can also contribute to feeling like you can't fully claim your success and achievement. When *The Lost Flowers of Alice Hart* was published in 2018, it was, to my bewildered delight, loved by readers, and did well sales-wise. Along with utter elation and disbelief, my heart often pounded painfully with anxiety, waiting for the moment the curtain would come down, so to speak. It wasn't so much that I felt like a fraud. It was more that the success was just so extraordinary that it seemed unbelievable to me. Something so joyful and so good couldn't possibly happen to me and my writing. I remember talking to Sam about it and saying, 'I think I need to be prepared for when this all ends.' Part of me was sectioned off from fully enjoying it all. It seemed important that

I held some of myself back so I could be braced for it all to fade, and for my love of writing to be taken away from me.

What happened with my debut novel was a rarity — something that every person who knew anything about writing or publishing would constantly tell me. 'This never happens,' they'd say. Other than trying my best to understand and accept that this success was happening to me, and to celebrate the joy of it when I could (which, it's important to say, I did), overall, the only tool I seemed to have to manage the experience was to resist being fully on board. Looking back now, I understand that I had no reason or previous experience to allow me to trust where this wild ride was taking me. I didn't know how to belong to the experience. How to claim it. Part of coping with the enormous joy of it was to keep part of myself at arm's length from it.

When it came time for my first artist date, I studied the instructions in *The Artist's Way* as if I was prepping for an exam: 'An artist date is a block of time … especially set aside and committed to nurturing your creative consciousness, your inner artist. In its most primary form, the artist date is an excursion, a play date that you pre-plan and defend against all interlopers. You do not take anyone on this artist date but you and your inner artist, a.k.a. your creative child.'

I gave myself the whole day. Washed my hair, chose what to wear, favouring joyful colours – my favourite olive-green velvet blazer with a soft pink floral print – and caught a bus into Manchester city centre. On the ride I was excited, imagining all the inspiration I was going to feel, and the wonders I was going to notice through the lenses of my I'm-on-an-artist-date goggles. I would go to the gallery and library and bookshop and let my inner artist run wild, soaking up all the creative inspiration and goodness possible.

When I arrived in the city, I got off the bus, stood on the edge of the street at Piccadilly Gardens ... and felt suddenly and completely lost. Not in a literal sense. In the sense that I was on an obstacle course and had lost my grip of the guide rope. I was flailing. All my excitement was gone. My day just felt silly. I was in the city, alone, and why? Because I was being an artist? Who was I to spend a day that way? My shoulders curled inwards.

But I stuck to my plan and headed in the direction of the Manchester Art Gallery. On the walk there, my mind filled with more intrusive thoughts. By the time I arrived, I felt like a wanker of unquantifiable proportions. Not only because of the riot my inner critic was having in my mind about the pointlessness of 'dating my creativity', but also because once I was out in the world with my aim to stimulate and nurture my creative desires and pleasures, I had absolutely no idea what I was doing. I stood in the foyer of the gallery trying to look like I belonged there, but I didn't know why I was there. I didn't know what to look at or how or why I'd ever thought being there would bring me creative pleasure. I certainly couldn't remember in that moment how to think for pleasure. I was frozen by my own internal harsh judgement.

I hadn't learned yet that I could take a deep breath, sit in the Pre-Raphaelite gallery and enjoy people-watching, allowing myself to wonder about the young person in purple gumboots or the elderly person with long, perfectly braided white hair. Or to notice how the light slanted through the gallery skylight, or to study the brushstrokes that created the iridescence in Frederick Richard Pickersgill's 1850 painting *A Little Gondelay*. Instead, on my first artist date, anxiety took hold of me. I got so caught up in knots about *doing* my artist date that I couldn't let myself explore and ponder or just *be* on my artist date. The combined sense of my foolishness and incompetence merged with the commentary of my inner critic and reduced me to defeat. I was no writer. I was just a try-hard. An imposter.

I scurried out of the gallery and walked for blocks through the city until the heat of shame on my face cooled. Ducked into Primark, a department store, for distraction – if I remember correctly, I tried on a pair of pineapple-shaped sunglasses – and then into a nearby café. I ordered a peppermint tea and let it go cold while I tried not to drown in humiliation of my own making. Even though Julia Cameron had warned me it would be uncomfortable to take my creativity on a date, I had no idea how much prioritising my curiosity and creativity would intimidate and threaten me. Everything about what I was doing – trying to recover a sense of myself as a creative person and a writer – felt ridiculous.

As I sat in the café with my cold tea, I gazed through the window, across the street to the shopfront of Fred Aldous, a large and beloved art and craft shop in Manchester. There was a flicker of something in my heart. I left the café and crossed the street.

Wandering through Fred Aldous, I strolled between the shelves. The air smelled like waxy crayons and ink and paper. I paused to run my hands over the notebooks, the pens, the stamps and stickers. The enamel badges, the sticks of coloured chalk, the velvet curtains of the photo booth in the corner. A shop assistant asked me if they could help me find anything. I shook my head. 'There's a lower level too,' they told me, pointing to the stairs I hadn't noticed. I went downstairs and found myself in a vast stationery wonderland of more cardboard, paper, pens, pencils, tools and textiles. Part of me was elated and delighted. The other part of me didn't know what I was doing there. I wasn't a *real* artist.

I left, deflated.

The following week, for my next artist date, I took more care with my planning: I wouldn't give myself the whole day, just a morning. I would go to my favourite wing in Manchester Art Gallery – not the whole gallery, just my favourite wing of it – and spend mindful time with the paintings I loved. Being curious, open, aware. Then – and this made me wriggle with joy – I promised myself I'd go to the gallery gift shop and take time to look at every little thing.

That day, I stood in front of some of my favourite paintings and looked at them in a way I hadn't before. Slowly. With curiosity. And imagination. What had Dante Gabriel Rossetti's paint palette looked like? What did the room where John William Waterhouse painted look like? What paintings might be hanging in front of me if Rossetti's and Waterhouse's female contemporaries had had the same access and opportunities to paint?

Later, I bought a notebook and a pen from the gallery gift shop, sat at a corner table in the gallery café and ordered myself a pot of tea to sip while I turned through the new, empty pages. I wrote about the imagined lives of the people I'd just observed around me in the gallery. Which paintings they'd paid attention to, and why. I found that the more I wrote, the more I had to write. I didn't feel like a fraud. I felt the way I'd felt as a seven-year-old at my writing desk. Absorbed. Content. Bewildered by what I didn't know about what my mind could do, until I started writing.

I didn't realise the time until I looked up through the high café windows and noticed the light had changed. I didn't even mind the crammed rush-hour bus ride home. I stood in the aisle, smiling to myself. In the parched dirt of my inner country, a seed had twitched and split open.

Thanks to *The Artist's Way* course, countless hours of therapy, and learning from other artists, writers and creative thinkers, now when I feel like I'm an imposter or fraud in my own life, I've come to understand that I've fallen out of a core sense of belonging to myself. That's what imposter syndrome is to me: feeling like I don't belong. And the remedy is fostering a sense of belonging.

When I feel like I'm outside myself and my creativity, as if I've shown up at a party I'm not invited to, I know that I need to reset. I need to get my footing right – stable, safe – and remember whose inner country I belong to. Whose house? My house.

In a 1973 interview with Bill Moyers, Maya Angelou said, 'You are only free when you realise you belong no place – you belong every place – no place at all. The price is high. The reward is great … I belong to myself. I'm very proud of that.'

The first time I read this, it made my brain freeze, as if I'd taken too big a mouthful of ice cream. How was it possible to belong nowhere and everywhere?

After I listened to Brené Brown answer an interview question about belonging, I started to get it. 'I belong everywhere I go, no matter where it is or who I'm with, as long as I never betray myself. The minute I become who you want me to be to fit in and make sure people like me is the moment I no longer belong anywhere. And that is hard … That's an everyday practice. Because I can be whoever you want me to be …'

When it comes to feeling like an imposter in my creativity, or when I feel like I'm not *really* a writer, I nurture and practise my sense of belonging. I remind myself that I belong in this room; I wrote this room. I belong in this life. This life is mine. I belong in this body. This body belongs to me. Practising belonging is, in any doubtful moment, choosing over and over again, no matter where I am or who I'm with, to accompany myself – to stay with myself, in my body – rather than abandon myself.

In 2015, I finished writing the first draft of my first novel, *The Lost Flowers of Alice Hart* – something I had long believed I was never going to be good enough to do. Holding the first print-out of the complete manuscript in my hands was a defining moment. I was thirty-five years old.

Before I wrote *Alice Hart*, I'd never been even slightly tempted to get a tattoo. There was no symbol or visual concept I could envisage that meant enough to me to ever mark my skin with. Some context: I came of age on the Gold Coast in the 1990s. To go through those years of nightclubbing every weekend in Surfers Paradise and make it out clean-skinned, without a butterfly tattoo on my hip or a dolphin tattoo on my lower back, feels now like some sort of small miracle. This is not a judgement of anyone who might have those tattoos. It is an expression of genuine surprise that, especially with my love of butterflies and the ocean, I do not have them.

After I finished the first draft of *Alice Hart*, I woke up one morning with a hot, almost burning sensation in my right forearm. The idea was immediate and clear: I wanted a tattoo. To celebrate the joy and the power I felt at having written from my heart. At having proved the commentary in my mind wrong.

I told a friend at the time about my urge. 'But what if it doesn't get published?' she asked me with apologetic concern. 'What if it gets rejected and never becomes a book and you have a tattoo of that failure on your skin forever?' It sounds harsh but it was a beautiful question to be asked because it prompted my immediate, gut-led answer. 'Publication isn't why I wrote it,' I said. Creating Alice's story, a story that didn't exist outside my mind and body in tangible form before I wrote it, was my reason. Heeding the one thing I'd known about myself to be true and unchanged since I was three was my reason. And, unlike scars on my skin from the actions of others, choosing to decorate my body, choosing to mark my body because of joy, *because I wanted to*, was my reason.

While I was on the tattoo table with my extraordinary tattooist, Samantha Smith, inking my first tattoo on my right forearm, every time I glanced down, it felt like I was seeing something inside me being revealed rather than being added to my skin. Under the needle of Sam's tattoo gun, my mind wandered back to when I played Dorothy in my Grade Five school play of *The Wizard of Oz*.

I was overcome by how good it felt to be at home in my body and, simultaneously, how unfamiliar that feeling was to me. Dorothy really knew her shit: there's no place like it.

Tattooing my body to celebrate and commemorate the realisation of my lifelong dream – to write a book, to be a writer – and to adorn myself with symbols and a story that I chose was a powerful way to take agency of my body. Because I wanted to do that with myself. Because I knew, finally, that I belonged to myself. Being tattooed after writing *The Lost Flowers of Alice Hart* was a coming-full-circle moment in my life. A homecoming. And a powerful lesson in belonging.

No matter what imposter syndrome tells us, creativity is not an exclusive clubhouse that we can't enter. It's not for a chosen few. It's not for just the 'good' ones who *really* deserve to belong there. Hannah Diviney, a leading writer and disability and women's rights advocate, writes: 'I've wanted to be a writer since I was four years old. That's the age I first figured out the power of a story. A power that isn't beamed down from the sky … and doesn't conjure things from thin air, fully formed, but instead lives inside people. Lives inside me. It's the closest thing the little girl inside me … has ever found to magic.' Hannah says that as she's grown older, she's realised that it's not only writers who can access this power; it dwells in creativity. Anyone who dares to create can have access to this magic.

To counter imposter syndrome by asserting that we belong wherever and however we create is to hold our torch of hopefulness high. To drag shame and cynicism and fear into its light. Even when our arms quiver from the strain. As singer and songwriter Nick Cave wrote, 'Hopefulness is the warrior emotion that can lay waste to cynicism. [It] says the world is worth believing in.'

At the beginning of 2020, when the world was locking down during the pandemic, Sam and I were in Australia. We'd come home from England in December 2019, for Christmas, and for me to work on *Back to Nature*. By April, when it became clear that we wouldn't be returning to England, I was devoured by anxiety. Not only because of what was happening in the world and around all of us, but additionally because I'd just signed a two-book contract with my publishers. And years of research for my second novel, *The Seven Skins of Esther Wilding*, was (and still is) gathering dust on a bookshelf in my Manchester office, 17,000 kilometres away. My mind was as slow as cold molasses to process this, and also to understand that I wouldn't be taking the research trips I'd booked to Denmark and the Faroe Islands. Instead, as Covid shut the world down, we were suddenly, indefinitely and very gratefully, living with my folks … where I had no space to work and write, and would have to start afresh with Esther Wilding's story. Writing from almost nothing.

Looking for solace, I returned to Elizabeth Gilbert. Something she wrote about the work of the poet Jack Gilbert (no relation) struck me, about the importance of delight, enjoyment and 'stubborn gladness in the ruthless furnace of this world'. I wondered if I could create a sense of delight and enjoyment around writing my second novel at a time when creating anything new felt, in countless ways and for countless reasons, impossible.

A few days later, I was at the kitchen table with Sam searching on the internet for places I might rent to write and work in, despairing over the cost and complications of staying anywhere else during lockdown. I began to feel the creep of overwhelm, trying to find a space that would allow me to work full-time while also staying close to my family in some kind of Covid-free safety bubble. In the middle of my research and rising stress, Mum came in from the garden and dropped some general motherly genius as she breezed past: 'Holls, what about a caravan?'

Cue frenzied internet searches and a lot of gasping and honking exclamations. Forty-eight hours later, I became the owner of a 1968 Olympic Riviera caravan, named Frenchie, to use as my writing office.

Since we pulled into the driveway with Frenchie in tow, there hasn't been a second that I've regretted or questioned buying her, which was a huge deal for me. With full acknowledgement of my privilege in being financially able to buy Frenchie, doing so was a powerful lesson in investing in myself. It's taken me the best part of a decade to unlearn patterns of self-deprivation and scarcity mindsets instilled in me by fear and violence. Making myself small was a deeply ingrained safety measure.

Holly's caravan, Frenchie, in situ

Buying Frenchie for the sole purpose of giving myself the space to write *Esther Wilding* at the beginning of the pandemic was transformative in a number of ways. One was how motivating and meaningful the act of buying her was. I was giving myself and my writing the space that I needed to do my job, to write Esther's story, to create a dedicated place where both of us could belong. Another was the sheer joy, wonder and sense of play that having Frenchie in my life brought me. Whether it was working with Sam to kit her out as my writing office, potting a flower garden around her with my parents, or spending hours inside with my dogs at my feet as I set up my writing desk, Frenchie was a source of deep and powerful joy.

As the world closed down and anxiety and fear were rife, I tended this little caravan brimming with plants, flowers and Esther's unwritten story. It kept me going.

Since then, when writing feels especially hard, or if I return to my desk after a long time away, I still sometimes don't know how to find my way in. To belong to myself or the story I'm writing. Over decades I've realised it's a similar devotion to how we care for someone we love. It's an act of tending. An offering of tenderness. I find my way back by taking extra care to make my workspace feel like a place where I want to be. A place where I feel like I belong. I remind myself to fly my *Fuck Saving Things for a Rainy Day* flag, and use my favourite notebooks and best pens, brew decadent tea and stir in ample spoonfuls of what I call my 'special occasion' honey (from the blossoms of blue gums in Lutruwita/Tasmania). The day, time, occasion, as we are all so keenly aware, is now.

Frenchie is the peak of my writing-space dreams. In the past, my spaces and resources were different. At one time my writing desk was pale-green chiffon covering a desk made of plywood and crates in a share house. In another share house it was a picnic blanket and cushions I'd lay out in the shade of an old, giant mango tree. In yet another share house, a Vancouver basement apartment, my writing desk was inside a wardrobe (I channelled as many Narnia vibes as I could). In my house in the desert, my writing desk faced a view of my garden filled with pukara/ thryptomene and my patio beneath the wide sky.

There's been at least one thing about every space I've made for writing that has been somehow welcoming, that has told me, *You belong here*. It didn't always mean I wrote or created anything, but it did mean that I knew that there was a space in the outside world that I'd made specifically for everything unwritten in my inside world. My inner country. Making space for my writing, even when I felt more like a fraud with nothing to say than a writer full of words, was a lifeline for my creativity and my sense of belonging. Each of those desks was a light for me that never went out.

A sense of belonging doesn't have to mean a vintage caravan. Or even a desk. It's about paying attention to the things, little and big, that cause your soul to strike flint and spark. That you recognise

However you can, light yourself up.

as signs of homecoming. Belonging. Belonging to yourself. It could be a new pen with glossy black ink. Or a bottle of clary sage essential oil. A scarf all the colours of the moon. A tattoo. A new notebook. Wearable art. A packet of wildflower seeds. Finding ten minutes a day to daydream. Whatever your soul hungers for. Recognise these things. Claim them. However you can, give these things to yourself. However you can, light yourself up.

What if you're not an imposter? What if you're not a fraud or a phony or an anomaly? What if you're hopeful? What if your imagination really is *your* house? *Your* inner country? What if you're welcome here and there? What if the creative ideas that call you, flaming at the edges from the force of your wonder and awe, are not flukes? What if Picasso was right when he said, 'Everything you can imagine is real'? What if you belong to creativity and creativity belongs to you? What if you belong here?

I find it helpful to remember no one is immune to imposter syndrome. And that no matter how it may seem or look from the outside, the challenge of feeling like we belong is an experience we all have. Even world-famous actors feel like frauds sometimes:

'Over the years, the stakes have become higher for me. Sometimes I wake up in the morning before going off to a shoot, and I think, *I can't do this; I'm a fraud.*' – Kate Winslet

'I go through [acute imposter syndrome] with every role. I think winning an Oscar may in fact have made it worse. *Now I've achieved this, what am I going to do next? What do I strive for?* Then I remember that I didn't get into acting for the accolades, I got into it for the joy of telling stories.' – Lupita Nyong'o

'No matter what we've done, there comes a point where you think, *How did I get here? When are they going to discover that I am, in fact, a fraud and take everything away from me?*' – Tom Hanks

'I have this constant fear that I'm a fraud and that I'm going to be found out.' – Michelle Pfeiffer

'You think, *Why would anyone want to see me again in a movie? And I don't know how to act anyway, so why am I doing this?*' – Meryl Streep

To assert that we're not imposters, that we do belong to and with ourselves and our creativity – nowhere and everywhere – takes great courage and action. I love what Kemi Nekvapil, author, coach and speaker, says about this: 'I think the idea that we overcome fear is an illusion ... For me it was, and still is, very much about taking action, any action, towards what we want. If I sat around waiting for fear to go, I would never do anything. Fear can be the driving force, the edge that is needed to take the leap.'

You might be fearful of how it might feel to you to claim your belonging. And yet the instinct is still inside you. To nest. To make a space where you and your creativity belong. A space all your own, that feels good, that is comfortable. Even if it's in a wardrobe.

In making and taking up this space, you're not answerable to anyone else's sense of belonging but your own. Your creativity. Maybe it's crates and plywood. Maybe it's fairy lights. Maybe it's pink velour. Maybe it's a hot desk, a share office. A corner café table. Tending Frenchie reminds me: creating dedicated physical space in our exterior lives for our mysterious inner lives is a sacred and powerful act. One that unequivocally says, *You belong here.*

Wherever it is, that space, make it yours. For you and your creativity to dwell, to cultivate joy, and to bring to the outside the wonders of your inner country.

Make it yours. You belong there. Here.

You belong.

IMPOSTER SYNDROME + YOU BELONG HERE PROVOCATIONS

Do you feel at home spending time in your inner country and imagination, or does it feel like a distant, abandoned, overgrown ruin?

What might it feel like to step back into that space or place and reclaim it as your own?

How might you foster a greater sense of belonging in your creativity?

Is there an object, a scent, something visual or audible, that you could bring into your creative space to encourage you to remember that you belong to your creativity, and it belongs to you?

What actions can you take to light up the joy and comfort of belonging in your creative process?

They say that 'home is where the heart is'. I think it is where the house is.

EMILY DICKINSON

EPILOGUE

Homecoming

I've never been great at handling goodbyes with anyone or anything I love. The surge of emotion and the bittersweetness of vulnerability in the closing moment of farewells often overwhelm me. I'm finding writing this conclusion to be similar. But there are still some things I want to share, words I want to leave you with.

Whatever you have or haven't created in the past five, ten, twenty, thirty years, you and your creativity are still, always, worthy. No matter how loud or strong the noise and resistance in your mind is to this truth, you are enough. You have what you need to answer the call of your inner country. You have what you need to start creating, exactly as you are today. And the same applies to tomorrow. And the day after that.

It's a shaky thing living a creative life, which is a feeling life. Living open to grief and open to joy. But you're never ever as alone in your feelings as you think you are. This book sees you. I see you. There are whole communities of people who feel like you do. If you can summon the courage to let your creativity guide you, or share your art, you'll find those people. That connection is waiting for you, if you just let yourself love what you love, and create it.

It took a reckoning with trauma and deep grief to shake me free of the trap fear had me in. I hope this is never the case for you. I hope you find the courage and conviction to give yourself permission to start answering the stirrings in your heart without suffering. And if you're already answering the call from your inner country to create, I hope your courage and conviction are evergreen.

Living a feeling life, it doesn't take much to be crushed under the weight of grief and tragedy in the world. While working hard for sadly necessary causes, and to fight horrific injustices and to save our beautiful planet and each other, it can be so easy to forget sometimes to also soak up and engage in the wonders of life, this random gift of being alive. Right now … and now … and now. It's unfathomable and at the same time true: during our deepest suffering and difficulty, delight and magic and beauty and joy are still around us.

What I try to remember is that in times of smallness and fear, the only antidote I've ever found is to breathe and live more, love more. Now is the perfect time to feel the way a cool breeze touches your bare skin. To notice the hues of light falling through the branches of the casuarina tree in your garden or trees in your local park; the feeling of a page turned by your thumb in a book; the smell of honey myrtle oil diffusing over a tealight candle in your oil burner; the look of joy and love on the face of someone waiting for you when they see you arrive; the first crunchy-chewy, syrupy, buttery bite of an Anzac biscuit warm from the oven. These tiny, miraculous, powerful pleasures of being alive.

I beg you, please take that class or write that story or sing that song or take that trip or hike that path. Please tell yourself you love who you are or are becoming. Please get that tattoo or build that shack or go to that concert or apply for that thing. If you think you've failed at being creative, please create again. Please keep creating. Because we can. Because we love how creativity makes us feel. How it connects us. Because we are breathing. Because we are alive.

Creating anything despite fear is how we learn to believe in ourselves and our creativity. It's how we try. It's how we unblock and recover our creative lives.

Take the little step. Make the time. Put your phone down in your idle moments and practise daydreaming instead. Do it today and again tomorrow. Step by step and day by day. It's a lesson I will be practising all my life, I think, taking little steps, and understanding that each and every one is an act of transformation. Every step changes us and our relationship with our creativity.

If we don't nurture our creativity, it's not good for us. Remember what Brené Brown said about unused creativity, 'It metastasizes. It turns into grief, rage, judgment, sorrow, shame.' When we avoid the discomfort of taking the first little step towards what we want to create, we also deny ourselves the magic that comes afterwards: of going inwards, reconnecting with and remembering what we love and why, and remembering where the light comes from on our inner country.

The little steps we take towards giving ourselves permission to create can be as pleasurable and joyous as we want to make them. We don't have to struggle or suffer or come from scarcity to create. You can make creating feel as good as you want to let it feel. Even if you're heartbroken. Especially if you're heartbroken.

Tend to yourself and your creativity with as much care as you would give to fostering the creativity of a young child or a beloved friend. Your hopes and dreams are worth your care, respect and nourishment.

We don't have to feel ready, or whole, or good, or enough, to start creating. We are living multiple truths in every single moment of our multifaceted lives. The vast depths and rich complexities that we all carry within us, most of which might not be obvious from the outside, can be a source of power. We can feel:

brave

terrified

anxious

strong

messy

organised

wounded

powerful

joyful

sad

traumatised

loving

disorganised

grounded

and fucking gloriously creative

ALL AT THE SAME TIME.

Whenever you feel overwhelmed and can't create, please remember that there's power in stepping away from the process and, especially, taking yourself into nature. Even if it's not something you do often. We are a species, part of the natural world. We all benefit, in ways we might not fully be aware of, from time spent in forests, under trees, by the sea or rivers, in deserts, and in city green spaces and gardens. Our health – our creativity – is connected to our relationship with the natural world. Oliver Sacks, author, doctor and neurologist, said, 'My religion is nature. That's what arouses those feelings of wonder and mysticism and gratitude in me.'

Our imagination and senses are always absorbing the environment we're in. Next time you feel stuck in your creativity, I hope you'll take yourself outdoors and experience a moment when the sky surprises you, or the wind brings you a welcome memory. When you notice the wild beauty of a magpie's throat vibrating as she sings, or a tree reminds you that change and growth are always happening, no matter how slow it may feel.

Hilma af Klint, the visionary Swedish artist, who went long unacknowledged for her work and only recently has become globally recognised, is known to have included in her creative process the act of automatic drawing and writing while communing and channelling with spirits through seances. In one of her notebooks, Klint wrote a piece entitled 'September 16, 1903'. While it's unknown whether Klint channelled or composed these words, they speak directly of the trust and commitment creativity demands of us and remind us that even when we think we're not making progress, there is always new growth happening, as in nature:

You are bewildered by what we have told you, but the phenomenon we are trying to explain is truly bewildering. What is this phenomenon, you ask? Well, beloved, it is that which we want to call the secret growing. How often have we heard you say that everything is futile, that nothing comes of all your labors. Yet like amorphous buds your endeavors sprout in all directions. You see everything as formless and you forget that this is a sign of life. Gradually the formlessness takes on more precise contours and the steadily growing roots feed an ever stronger plant, which will one day explode with an abundance of leaves and flowers.

Just like the seasons and cycles of many trees, plants, flowers, animals and insects, it's in our DNA to thrive and bloom. When my heart is broken, when my mind's a mess, when I feel happy, when I feel peaceful – however I am – my relationship with my creativity is bettered by nature. It's a wisdom our bodies know, carried in our blood. I descend from Celtic and Scandinavian people, and some of my ancestors were Welsh. One of my favourite pieces of Welsh language in the brief time I've been researching is *Dod yn ôl at fy nghoed*, which translates as 'To return to my trees'. Meaning to come back to your senses, to return to a steady and grounded state of mind.

May we fill our inner country with the wonders from the natural world.

May we feel the terror of trusting in ourselves and our creativity, and bloom anyway.

You are allowed to create for joy.

You are allowed to dress for joy.

You are allowed to write for joy.

You are allowed to cook for joy.

You are allowed to research for joy.

You are allowed to sew for joy.

You are allowed to paint for joy.

You are allowed to dance for joy.

You are allowed to sing for joy.

You are allowed to love for joy.

You are allowed to communicate for joy.

You are allowed to garden for joy.

You are allowed to compose for joy.

You are allowed to dream for joy.

You are allowed to photograph for joy.

You are allowed to gather for joy.

You are allowed to adorn yourself for joy.

You are allowed to start creating at any time in your life for joy.

Your joy is the reason.

Your joy is the reason.

Your joy is the reason.

Imagination is a powerful gift given to human beings. It provides endless pleasure and we never grow out of enjoying it, no matter how adulthood may lead us to think otherwise. Creativity is a power that connects us more deeply with ourselves and each other. When we stop ourselves from engaging in our creativity, we suffer. Author and anthropologist Zora Neale Hurston wrote, 'There are years that ask questions and years that answer.' Maybe you've been asking yourself for years if you can create. If it's something you can do. Maybe it's been years since you were last creative and you're asking yourself if it's too late to create again. Maybe you're in a creative block, asking yourself if you'll ever have an idea that you love again.

Let this be the year you answer.

Creativity is a process, and so is learning to give ourselves permission to create and prioritise the joy that creating brings us. Little step by little step.

You have the courage to begin. To continue.

Whenever you and your creativity need it, I hope you give yourself what you need to return to your trees. I wish you a deeply joyous journey.

When I decided to write this book, most of me feared I could not do it. But there was a strong and curious voice in my mind that asked, *What if I can?* It's been my focus every time I've faltered while writing and resolved to keep going. *What if I can?*

So I ask you, my dear reader, what if you can?

What if you can?

I know.

But what if you can?

Truth: the choice to create because we love to do it is ours. The inner country of creativity and the house that joy built there are ours.

Truth: it's always fearful. Always joyful.

Truth: the light is always left on. Always guiding. Always waiting for us to come back to ourselves.

Welcome home.

You are allowed to create for joy. Your joy is the reason.

ENDNOTES

Epigraph

13   'I am out with lanterns, looking for myself': Emily Dickinson, letter
from Dickinson to Elizabeth Holland, 20 January 1856, in *The
Letters of Emily Dickinson*, edited by Thomas H. Johnson, Associate
Editor, Theodora Ward, Cambridge, Mass.: The Belknap Press
of Harvard University Press, Copyright © 1958 by the President
and Fellows of Harvard College. Copyright © renewed 1986 by
the President and Fellows of Harvard College. Copyright © 1914,
1924, 1932, 1942 by Martha Dickinson Bianchi. Copyright ©
1952 by Alfred Leete Hampson. Copyright © 1960 by Mary L.
Hampson. Used by permission. All rights reserved.

Prologue: A Light Left On

17   'Out on the wastes of the Never Never': Barcroft Boake, 'Where
the Dead Men Lie', in *Where the Dead Men Lie, and Other Poems*,
Sydney: Angus & Robertson, 1897.

21 *'the misconception that women'*: Sharon Doane, *New Beginnings: A Creative Writing Guide for Women Who Have Left Abusive Partners*, Cambridge, Mass.: Da Capo Press, 1996.

23 *shame thrives on secret-keeping*: Brené Brown, *Daring Greatly: How the Courage to Be Vulnerable Transforms the Way We Live, Love, Parent and Lead*, London: Penguin, 2013.

23 *'And All of us … in the Land of the Never-Never'*: Mrs Aeneas (Jeannie) Gunn, *We of the Never-Never*, Sydney: Angus & Robertson, 1908, pp.xi–xii. Used by permission of the estate of Jeannie Gunn and HarperCollins Publishers Australia Pty Ltd.

24 *'A radiance is inside us'*: Anne Lamott, *Stitches: A Handbook on Meaning, Hope and Repair*, London: Hodder & Stoughton, 2014.

26 *'to taste life twice'*: Anaïs Nin, *Trapeze: The Unexpurgated Diary of Anaïs Nin, 1947–1955*, San Antonio: Sky Blue Press, 2017.

27 *'second to the right, and straight on till morning'*: J.M. Barrie, *Peter Pan: Peter and Wendy*, Ettelbrück, Luxembourg: Outlook Verlag, 2019 (reproduction of the original 1911 publication).

30 *anything that goes unsaid acquires the importance of a scream:* Luisa Valenzuela, 'Dangerous Words', trans. Cynthia Ventura, *Review of Contemporary Fiction*, vol.6, no.3 (1986), p.10.

35 *'What did you do as a child'*: Carl Jung, quoted in Anna Potter, *Flower Philosophy: Seasonal Projects to Inspire and Restore*, London: White Lion Publishing, 2023, p.164.

Introduction: Our House

41 *'the ability to feel wonder'*: Kae Tempest, *On Connection*, London: Faber & Faber, 2020, p.5.

41   *'You can't use up creativity'*: Maya Angelou, quoted in Mary
     Ardito, 'It's the thought that counts', *Bell Telephone Magazine*,
     vol.61, no.1 (1982), p.33.

42   *create whatever causes a revolution in your heart*: Elizabeth Gilbert, *Big
     Magic: How to Live a Creative Life, and Let Go of Your Fear*, New
     York: Bloomsbury, 2015, Part III.

42   *'Say yes and you'll figure it out afterwards'*: Tina Fey, quoted
     in Brett Blumenthal, *52 Small Changes for the Mind: Improve
     Memory, Minimize Stress, Increase Productivity, Boost Happiness*, San
     Francisco: Chronicle Books, 2015, p.155.

44   *'If you stop imagining things'*: Maria Dahvana Headley, 'Tell me
     a story: how fantastical literature has been shaped by storytellers
     and audiences', 2023 Tolkien Lecture, 16 May 2023,
     YouTube.

45   *'I will never apologise for embracing joy'*: Karen Walrond in
     conversation with Brené Brown, *Unlocking Us* podcast,
     brenebrown.com/podcast/accessing-joy-and-finding-connection-
     in-the-midst-of-struggle/#transcript

50   *'We Shake With Joy'*: Mary Oliver, *Evidence: Poems*, Boston:
     Beacon Press, 2009, p.13.

51   *'Whose house? Our house!'*: from *Friday Night Lights*, NBC,
     2006–2010.

1 Fear + Play: Raise Your Sword

63   *As explained by psychotherapist Astrid Burke*: Astrid Burke, 'The
     four Fs of complex trauma: recognizing and healing our survival
     strategies', Intuitive Healing website, 1 October 2020.

67   *born with two fears*: Nadia Kounang, 'What is the science behind fear?', *CNN Health*, CNN website, 29 October 2015.

68   *'I've always been absolutely terrified'*: Georgia O'Keeffe, quoted in Olivia Laing, 'The wild beauty of Georgia O'Keeffe', *The Guardian*, 1 July 2016.

69   *'Play is a range of intrinsically motivated activities'*: 'Play (activity)', Wikipedia.

69   *survey of animals, pleasure and play*: Jonathan Balcombe, 'Animal pleasure and its moral significance', *Applied Animal Behavior Science*, vol.118, no.3 (2009), pp.208–216.

69   *a male Cuban crocodile was observed*: Vladimir Dinets, 'Play behavior in crocodilians', *Animal Behavior and Cognition*, vol.2, no.1 (2015), pp.49–55.

70   *ravens have been observed 'snowboarding'*: 'All fur and games: Why do animals play?', BBC Earth website, n.d.

70   *'When playing, an animal usually tries'*: Irene Lobato Vila, 'Why do animals play?', All You Need Is Biology website, 9 April 2016.

71   *'kills the spirit and stunts mental growth'*: Peter Gray, *Free to Learn: Why Unleashing the Instinct to Play Will Make Our Children Happier, More Self-Reliant, and Better Students for Life*, New York: Basic Books, 2013, Chapter 1.

72   *'use your hands'*: Austin Kleon, *Steal Like an Artist: 10 Things Nobody Told You about Being Creative*, New York: Workman Publishing, 2022, p.54.

Endnotes

2 Self-doubt + Self-compassion: An Ancient Beauty

83   *'The worst enemy to creativity is self-doubt'*: Sylvia Plath, *The Journals of Sylvia Plath*, New York: Knopf Doubleday Publishing Group, 2013, p.85.

87   *'the time comes when the risk of remaining tight'*: See Elizabeth Appell, 'Anaïs Nin and I are in lock step', Elizabeth Appell blog, December 2012.

89   *'Self-compassion is one of the most powerful sources'*: Kristin Neff, Self-Compassion, www.self-compassion.org

98   *'If you hear a voice within you say'*: Vincent van Gogh, letter to his brother, Theo van Gogh, in Robert Harrison (ed. and trans.), *Letters of Vincent van Gogh to His Brother, 1872–1886*, vol.2, London: Constable & Company, 1927, p.332.

98   *'Cherry Blossoms'*: Toi Derricotte, 'Cherry Blossoms', *The Undertaker's Daughter*, Pittsburgh: University of Pittsburgh Press, 2011, pp.78–79.

3 Failure + Nothing is Wasted: The Door to the Wild

107   *creativity and innovation require us to stop obsessing about 'failure'*: Peter Sims, 'The no.1 enemy of creativity: fear of failure', *Harvard Business Review*, 5 October 2012.

114   *'In nature there is no such thing as garbage'*: Veena Sahajwalla, 'There's no such thing as waste', *Events*, UNSW Sydney website.

119   *'For he comes, the human child'*: W.B. Yeats, 'The Stolen Child', *The Wandering of Oisin and Other Poems*, London: Kegan Paul & Co., 1889.

120 *the hours pass like minutes*: Jung, op. cit.

120 *'If you have a deep scar'*: Clarissa Pinkola Estés, *Women Who Run with the Wolves: Myths and Stories of the Wild Woman Archetype*, New York: Random House, 1996, p.21.

4 Procrastination + Presence: An Overgrown Path

124 *'The truth will set you free, but first it will piss you off'*: Gloria Steinem, quoted in 'Sic transit gloria', *Heterodoxy: Articles and Animadiversions on Political Correctness and Other Follies*, vol.6, no.3 (1998), p.3.

125 *'You need to find a way to bring your body'*: Kleon, op. cit.

126 *a pattern in human behaviour called 'time inconsistency'*: James Clear, *Atomic Habits: An Easy and Proven Way to Build Good Habits and Break Bad Ones*, London: Penguin, 2018.

126 *'taking actions with long-term benefits'*: James Clear, 'Procrastination: A scientific guide on how to stop procrastinating', James Clear website.

126 *'I want it now!'*: In the film *Willy Wonka & the Chocolate Factory*, Paramount Pictures, 1971.

130 *In the world of donkey rehabilitation*: Ben Hart, 'Shaping behaviour: why small steps are the key to success', The Donkey Sanctuary website, 11 January 2022.

135 *When it comes to procrastination*: Clear, op. cit.

141 *love is a four-letter word*: Edith Eger, in Brené Brown, 'Brené with Dr. Edith Eger on recognizing the choices and gifts in our lives', *Unlocking Us* podcast, 2021, Brené Brown website.

143 *'We, who have lived in it, and loved it, and left it'*: Gunn, op. cit. Used by permission of the estate of Jeannie Gunn and HarperCollins Publishers Australia Pty Ltd.

5 Inner Critic + Inner Fan: Stay Gold

152 *'Most people don't know'*: Lauren Canonico, quoted in Margarita Tartakovsky, 'How to deal with an especially cruel inner critic', Psych Central website, 2 October 2018.

152 *'Their voice and perceptions of us become our voice'*: Christina Cruz, quoted in Tartakovsky, ibid.

153 *'hold ourselves to those same standards'*: Lauren Canonico, quoted in Tartakovsky, ibid.

153 *'seemingly confirm the inner critic's negative stance'*: Ibid.

160 *emotions are literally contagious*: Ed Batista, 'Brené Brown, vulnerability, empathy and leadership', Ed Batista Executive Coaching, 3 August 2014.

162 *'To find joy … to find hope'*: Maria Popova, 'Enchantment and the courage of joy: René Magritte on the antidote to the banality of pessimism', *The Marginalian*, 31 May 2023.

162 *uses 'compassionate inquiry' and 'a playful approach'*: See Ben Crowe, Mojo Crowe's Post, LinkedIn, June 2023, au.linkedin. com/posts/mojo-crowe_with-compassionate-inquiry-we-reshape-our-activity-7039672455489093633-5cZh

162 *'To be a fan means many things'*: Michael Bond, 'The big idea: why you should embrace your inner fan', *The Guardian*, 22 May 2023.

168 *'Stay gold, Ponyboy'*: S.E. Hinton, *The Outsiders*, New York: Penguin Young Readers Group, 2012.

6 Outer Critic + Resilience: We Can Be Starfish

173 *the advice Dame Helen Mirren says she would give to her younger self*:
Michelle Lee, 'Why Helen Mirren wishes she'd said "fuck off"
more as a young woman', *Allure*, 14 August 2017.

174 *'To escape criticism'*: Elbert Hubbard, *The Motto Book: Being a
Catalogue of Epigrams by Fra Elbertus (pseudonym of Elbert Hubbard),
Assisted at Times by Solomon, Ruskin, Shakespeare, and others*, East
Aurora: The Roycrofters, 1909, pp.38–39.

177 *'Unused creativity is not benign'*: Brené Brown, interviewed by
Oprah Winfrey, Come What May Productions, Facebook,
14 January 2021.

177 *'That's how I think of art'*: Ocean Vuong, in conversation with
Amy Rose Spiegel, 'On being generous in your work', The
Creative Independent website, 15 March 2022.

178 *'the expression of disapproval'*: 'Criticism' search on Google,
bringing up Oxford Languages definition from Oxford
University Press.

179 *not all emotions are of equal value to us*: Amrisha Vaish, Tobias
Grossmann & Amanda Woodward, 'Not all emotions are created
equal: the negativity bias in social-emotional development',
Psychological Bulletin, vol.134, no.3 (2008) pp.383–403,
doi:10.1037/0033-2909.134.3.383

183 *'It is not the critic who counts'*: Theodore Roosevelt, speech
at the Sorbonne, Paris, 23 April 1910, quoted in Brown,
op. cit., p.1.

185 *Ben Crowe talks about*: mojocrowe (Ben Crowe), Instagram,
2 June 2020, www.instagram.com/reel/Cs9dzHqPTLb

187 *'remember they were once a baby too'*: alokvmenon (Alok Vaid-Menon), Instagram, 11 June 2023, www.instagram.com/reel/CtUC5Xngk9A

188 *'Do what you feel in your heart to be right'*: Ann Atkins, *Eleanor Roosevelt – Unleashed: A Life of Soul Searching and Self Discovery*, Paoli, Penn.: Flash History Press, 2011.

188 *'Goddam it, FEELING is what I like in art'*: Jack Kerouac, in Ted Berrigan, 'Jack Kerouac, The Art of Fiction No.41,' *The Paris Review*, No.45 (Summer 1968).

189 *one-star reviews*: 1. Review of *To Kill a Mockingbird* by Azura, Goodreads, 19 February 2012, www.goodreads.com/review/show/263177113; 2. Review of *Wuthering Heights* by Andrea, Goodreads, 10 February 2009, www.goodreads.com/book/show/6185.Wuthering_Heights - CommunityReviews; 3. Review of The Beatles by William F. Buckley Jr, *Boston Globe*, 13 September 1964, see Cary Schneider, 'What the critics wrote about the Beatles in 1964', *Los Angeles Times*, 9 February 2014; 4. Review of *Dirty Dancing* by 'Anonymous', Rotten Tomatoes, 6 April 2015 (no longer available); 5. Review of *The Story of Peppa Pig* by Kiyoko, Goodreads, 1 May 2020, www.goodreads.com/book/show/15062997-the-story-of-peppa-pig - CommunityReviews; 6. Review of *Sleepless in Seattle* by Elise C., Rotten Tomatoes, 18 March 2023, www.rottentomatoes.com/m/sleepless_in_seattle/reviews?page=41&type=user; 7. Review of *E.T.* by character Perd Hapley, *Parks and Recreation*, Season 5, Episode 16, see 'Best of Perd Hapley', *Parks and Recreation* channel, YouTube, 15 August 2018, www.youtube.com/watch?v=UjX4_-IX-7E

191 '*At the end of the day, we can endure much more*': Frida Kahlo, quoted in Laura Almeida, 'Quotes from Frida Kahlo', Denver Art Museum, 28 December 2020.

192 '*I believe that maturity is not an outgrowing*': Ursula Le Guin, '106. A child who survived', *Ursula K. Le Guin Blog 106*, ursulakeleguin.com

7 Creative Block + Daydream Machine: Sniffing Pink Flamingo

202 '*The unfed mind devours itself*': Gore Vidal, quoted in Arthur Lubow, 'Gore's lore', *Vanity Fair*, September 1992.

202 '*Daydreaming has been under attack*': Alison Escalante, 'New research finds daydreaming is good for our health', *Forbes*, 23 March 2021.

202 '*This is part of our cognitive toolkit*': Erin Westgate in 'Why we're so bad at daydreaming, and how to fix it', *News*, University of Florida website, 4 March 2021.

203 '*you can harness in your everyday life*': Alisson Clark, 'Why we're so bad at daydreaming, and how to fix it', *University of Florida News*, 4 March 2021.

204 '*67% of men and 25% of women*': Ibid.

204 *Erin Westgate assures us*: Escalante, op. cit.

208 '*the ability to combine existing ideas*': Marcos Economides, 'How to overcome a creative block', Headspace, www.headspace.com

209 '*extends far beyond living memory*': 'Kanalaritja: An unbroken string', Tasmanian Museum and Art Gallery website, kanalaritja. tmag.tas.gov.au

212 *MRI brain scans of jazz musicians*: Charles J. Limb & Allen R. Braun, 'Neural substrates of spontaneous musical performance: An fMRI study of jazz improvisation', *PloS ONE*, vol.3, no.2 (27 February 2008).

218 *'Do you know what it is that you love?'*: Tabitha Carvan, *This Is Not a Book about Benedict Cumberbatch*, Sydney: HarperCollins, 2022. Used with the permission of the author.

8 Imposter Syndrome + You Belong Here: There's No Place Like It

222 *'Nothing can come of nothing'*: William Shakespeare, *King Lear*, Act 1, Scene 1.

222 *'Nothing changes if nothing changes'*: Karen Eisenbraun, 'What "nothing changes if nothing changes" means for your recovery', Alcoholics Resource Center website, 11 March 2022.

223 *'Is it very painful?'*: Michael Ende, *The Neverending Story*, trans. Ralph Manheim, New York: Puffin, 1983, p.57.

223 'The Artist's Way *provides a twelve-week course'*: Julia Cameron, *The Artist's Way: A Spiritual Path to Greater Creativity*, London: Souvenir Press, 2020.

224 *The term 'imposter syndrome'*: Pauline Rose Clance & Suzanne Imes, 'The impostor phenomenon in high achieving women: Dynamics and therapeutic intervention', *Psychotherapy: Theory, Research and Practice*, vol.15, no.3 (1978).

226 *'An artist date is a block of time'*: Julia Cameron, op. cit., p.18.

231 *'You are only free when you realise you belong no place'*: Maya Angelou, quoted in Bill Moyers, 'A conversation with Maya Angelou', Bill Moyers Journal website, 21 November 1973.

231 *'I belong everywhere I go'*: Brené Brown, *Deepstash* channel, YouTube.

234 *'I've wanted to be a writer since I was four years old'*: Hannah Diviney, 'Introducing Hannah Diviney', Cerebral Palsy Alliance website, 19 July 2021. Used with the permission of the author.

235 *'Hopefulness is the warrior emotion'*: Nick Cave, The Red Hand Files, no.190, April 2022.

236 *'stubborn gladness'*: Elizabeth Gilbert, quoted in Joe Fassler, 'The "stubborn gladness" of Elizabeth Gilbert's favorite poet', *The Atlantic*, 6 November 2013.

241 *'Everything you can imagine is real'*: Pablo Picasso, quoted at 'Pablo Picasso', Gagosian.

242 *'Over the years, the stakes'*: Kate Winslet, quoted in Kristin Shorten, 'High-achievers suffering from "imposter syndrome"', news.com.au, 10 December 2013.

242 *'I go through … with every role'*: Lupita Nyong'o, quoted in Tom Huddleston, 'Lupita Nyong'o: "If I'm having a Cinderella moment, why not enjoy the hell out of it?"', *Time Out*, 26 September 2016.

242 *'No matter what we've done'*: Tom Hanks, quoted in 'Tom Hanks says self-doubt is "a high-wire act that we all walk"', *Fresh Air*, NPR website, 26 April 2016.

242 *'I have this constant fear'*: Michelle Pfeiffer, quoted in Darren Aronofsky, 'Michelle Pfeiffer', *Interview*, 28 March 2017.

242 *'You think,* Why would anyone'*: Meryl Streep, quoted in Ken Burns, Interview with Meryl Streep, *USA Weekend*, 1 December 2002.

Endnotes

242   *'I think the idea that we overcome fear is an illusion'*: 'The Leap
Stories #43: Kemi Nekvapil' (interview with Kemi Nekvapil),
The Leap Stories, Of Kin website.

245   *'They say that "home is where the heart is"'*: letter, Emily Dickinson
to Elizabeth Holland, 20 January 1856, in *The Letters of Emily
Dickinson*, edited by Thomas H. Johnson, Associate Editor,
Theodora Ward, Cambridge, Mass.: The Belknap Press of
Harvard University Press, Copyright © 1958 by the President and
Fellows of Harvard College. Copyright © renewed 1986 by the
President and Fellows of Harvard College. Copyright © 1914,
1924, 1932, 1942 by Martha Dickinson Bianchi. Copyright ©
1952 by Alfred Leete Hampson. Copyright © 1960 by Mary L.
Hampson. Used by permission. All rights reserved.

250   *'It metastasizes. It turns into grief'*: Brené Brown, interviewed
by Oprah Winfrey, Come What May Productions, Facebook,
14 January 2021.

Homecoming

252   *'My religion is nature'*: Oliver Sacks, *Gratitude*, New York: Knopf,
2015.

253   *'You are bewildered by what we have told you'*: Hilma af Klint,
16 September 1903, in Christine Burgin (ed.), *Hilma af Klint:
Notes and Methods*, Chicago: University of Chicago Press, 2018,
p.29.

255   'There are years that ask questions': Zora Neale Hurston, *Their
Eyes Were Watching God*, J.B. Lippincott, Philadelphia.

ACKNOWLEDGEMENTS

This book was written with gratitude on unceded Bundjalung Country and Yugambeh Country, during the season when humpback whales migrate south and the wattle blooms. I extend my respect to the traditional owners of these lands and waterways, and to their families and ancestors, who have cared for these areas for thousands of years. I acknowledge them as the original storytellers of these regions.

My unending thanks to Catherine Milne, Head of Fiction at HarperCollins Australia, my publisher and friend, whose instinct and knowledge of stories make me better in every way. I didn't know (or maybe wouldn't acknowledge) that *The House That Joy Built* had been waiting, impatiently, for me to write it, until Catherine shone her proverbial torch on my inner country and said, THERE. Now, here it is. Such is the power that someone's incandescent belief and encouragement can have on our lives. Scott Forbes, my editor, I would not survive deadlines, or citations, or navigating the process of drawing stories from darkness into light without you. Thank you for showing me so astutely how and where to make my writing shine. Hazel Lam, every time I think you couldn't design a better cover, you come along, waving your *Challenge Accepted* banner, and render me speechless (no small feat). Thank you for finding the delicious, joyous, inviting art of Kate Dehler, and thank you for creating this exceptional cover. Edith Rewa, your illustrations are the stuff of dreams. Three books and counting: my words and your art. Is this a tradition?! (YES IT IS.) I am so grateful to have your creativity, love and friendship in my books and life. Alice Wood, to be in the vicinity of your magic, pom-poms, wisdom, skill and encouragement is transformative; thank you for being my incomparable Whiz. Lily, Hannah, Mark, Sean, KM, Erin, Kate, Bridge, Jim ... my whole team at HarperCollins, thank you for being my village, believing in my work and giving it and me your energy, time and resources. Many thanks also to Nicola Young, for copy editing, and Madeleine James, for proofreading.

It's been eight years since I sat on Skype(!) and met with Benython Oldfield and Sharon Galant of Zeitgeist Agency, after they'd read the first few chapters of *The Lost Flowers of Alice Hart*. Thank you, both, and Thomasin Chinnery, the fourth member of our War Room Team, for being my indefatigable champions.

My thanks to the family of Jeannie Gunn for giving me such generous permission to quote from *We of the Never-Never*, and

Acknowledgements

to Harvard University Press for their generous permission to use material from Emily Dickinson's letters – there couldn't be more perfect words to open and close this book with. I am deeply and thoroughly honoured.

Michaela Kalowski was the first person to read the early pages of this book, when I didn't know what it was and shook with nervous wonder that it might be something. Mink, thank you for your caps-lock texts, telling me how alight these words were in your heart. Your belief in my work gives me the courage to keep writing, to keep answering the stories that ask to come to the page.

My first readers and beloved circle scattered around the world – Myf Jones, Laura Donovan, Libby Morgan – thank you for holding unfailing space for me and my writing within the immeasurable capacities of your hearts. Thank you for telling me that these words mean something to you. When I think of who I'm writing for, I see your eyes and wicked grins. Zoe Rimmer, your friendship is a life-enriching joy that I treasure; thank you so much for your support, enthusiasm, love and generosity. Magic green soup forever. Special mention to Nanny Sparkles, Theresa Sainty, for her big-hearted encouragement.

Brooke Davis and Jeremy Lachlan, where would I be without Team WIICA? I don't ever want to know. Thank you for being my overarching trees that give me shelter and belonging, especially when I don't realise that I need them. There is nothing like being loved by you both.

Beloved family and friends, I'm no island. Thank you for being my sea.

I wrote this book in an unrelenting storm of work. I couldn't have stayed the course without your love and support, Mamaleen and Dadgee. Thank you for letting me sprawl through the house with my writing and ideas for the fourth unexpected year running. Being 'stuck' with you from 2020 onwards is one of the greatest gifts I'll have in this life. Mama, thank you for being my true north.

Neither of my novels was written without being aided by the superpowers of dogs and this new book is no exception. Goose, Teapot, Poppy, Frankie, Finnegan, you'll never read this but deserve every acknowledgement possible for your pure and unconditional love. Shout out to Little Feets for pure, unbridled love and joy.

Sam Harris. When I had no reason to trust or to believe that anything good might be ahead of me, I met you. Knowing the wonders of your mind and nature is a joy unlike any other I've ever felt and has changed my life more times than I can count. Thank you for telling me where you thought I might find the butterflies. Thank you for giving me what I didn't know I needed to build my own ladder and climb.

Dearest readers, since I was first published in 2018, you have responded to my books with embracing kindness and passion and a generosity of spirit that has undone me. An author is nothing without her readers. Thank you for being mine. Thank you for your courage and questions that planted the first seeds of this book. As ever, my gratitude is yours.

AUTHOR'S NOTE

As an accompaniment to *The House That Joy Built*, I've created a page on my website that's called *The Joy Rise*, where you can send me a question about creativity. Maybe you've been to an event with me and haven't been able to ask a question. Or maybe you've seen the Q&As I sometimes do on Instagram to talk about creativity, and you've missed a chance to participate. Or maybe you've finished reading this book and have something you'd like to ask me. *The Joy Rise* is a place for your questions about writing, fear, joy, courage, stories and creativity. I'll answer online and in my newsletter, which you can also subscribe to here: https://hollyringland.com/ask-holly-a-question

The pages of this book are filled with the generosity and care of countless people, especially a few who allowed me to share their stories and creative processes.

Libby Morgan is a meditation practitioner. You can find Libby's meditations (which make my body soften and often leave me nearly dribbling) at www.libbymorgan.com.au

Laura Donovan is a metalsmith, and the woman behind SilverGreen Jewellery. You can find Laura's evocative creations, of which I have a treasured many, at www.silvergreenjewellery.com

Zoe Rimmer is a Pakana (Tasmanian Aboriginal) woman, an academic, curator and artist. For information about her academic research, visit https://discover.utas.edu.au/Zoe.Rimmer/about; to learn more about Zoe's curatorial work and art, go to www.milangkani.com.au

RESOURCES

AUSTRALIA

Mental health

Lifeline
13 11 14, www.lifeline.org.au
Confidential telephone counselling.

SANE Australia helpline
1800 187 263, www.sane.org
Information about mental health issues and referrals.

Family violence crisis and support

NATIONAL

National Sexual Assault and Domestic Family
Violence Counselling Service
1800 RESPECT (1800 737 732), www.1800respect.org.au

AUSTRALIAN CAPITAL TERRITORY

Domestic Violence Crisis Service ACT
02 6280 0900, www.dvcs.org.au

NEW SOUTH WALES

Domestic Violence Line
1800 656 463, www.facs.nsw.gov.au/domestic-violence;
www.dvnsw.org.au/

NORTHERN TERRITORY

Dawn House
08 8945 1388, www.dawnhouse.org.au

QUEENSLAND

DV Connect Women's line
1800 811 811, www.dvconnect.org/womensline

Resources

SOUTH AUSTRALIA
Domestic Violence and Aboriginal Family Violence
Gateway Service
1800 800 098, elmplace.org.au

TASMANIA
Family Violence Response and Referral line
1800 633 937, www.safeathome.tas.gov.au/services

VICTORIA
Safe Steps Family Violence Response Centre
1800 015 188, www.safesteps.org.au

WESTERN AUSTRALIA
Women's Domestic Violence Helpline
08 9223 1188 or 1800 007 339, www.wa.gov.au/service/
community-services/community-support/womens-domestic-
violence-helpline

NEW ZEALAND

Mental health

Lifeline NZ

0800 543 354, mentalhealth.org.nz/links/link/lifeline-nz

Confidential telephone counselling.

Family violence crisis and support

Shine

0508 744 633, www.2shine.org.nz

Domestic abuse helpline for anyone living with abuse.

Family Violence Information Line

0800 456 450, www.areyouok.org.nz

Provides self-help information and connection to
appropriate services.

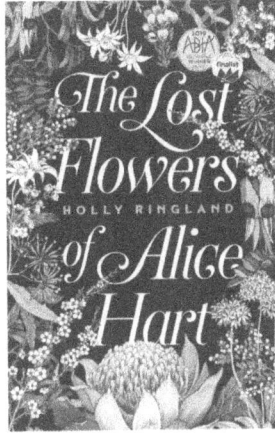

Winner of the 2019 ABIA General Fiction Book of the Year Award

The international bestseller, recently adapted into an Amazon Prime TV series, *The Lost Flowers of Alice Hart* tells the enchanting and compelling story of a young girl, daughter of an abusive father, who has to learn the hard way that she can break the patterns of the past, live on her own terms and find her own strength.

A young girl loses both her parents in a tragic event, and is taken to live with her grandmother on a flower farm. Growing up, Alice learns the language of Australian native flowers as a way to say the things that are too hard to speak. But she also learns that there are secrets within secrets about her past. An unexpected betrayal leaves her reeling, and she escapes to try to make her own – sometimes painful – way through the world, and to find her story.

The Lost Flowers of Alice Hart is a story about stories: those we inherit, those we select to define us, and those we decide to hide. It is a novel about the secrets we keep and how they haunt us, and the stories we tell ourselves in order to survive.

Spanning twenty years, and set between sugar cane fields by the sea, a native Australian flower farm and a celestial crater in the central desert, *The Lost Flowers of Alice Hart* follows the life of Alice as she discovers that the most powerful story she will ever possess is her own.

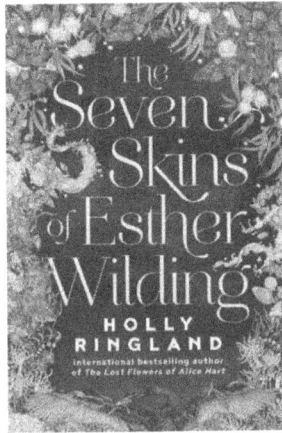

From international bestselling author of *The Lost Flowers of Alice Hart*, Holly Ringland, comes a haunting and magical novel about joy, grief, courage and transformation.

The last time Esther Wilding's beloved older sister Aura was seen, she was walking along the shore towards the sea. In the wake of Aura's disappearance, Esther's family struggles to live with their loss. To seek the truth about her sister's death, Esther reluctantly travels from Lutruwita, Tasmania to Copenhagen, and then to the Faroe Islands, following the trail of the stories Aura left behind: seven fairy tales about selkies, swans and women, alongside cryptic verses Aura wrote and had secretly tattooed on her body.

The Seven Skins of Esther Wilding is a sweeping, deeply beautiful and profoundly moving novel about the far-reaches of sisterly love, the power of wearing your heart on your skin, and the ways life can transform when we find the courage to feel the fullness of both grief and joy.